D1085847

THIS BOOK IS DEDICATED TO THE MEMORY OF

John J. Heney

Otto Kraushaar

Fred McCall

THE MUSIC OF HENRY FILLMORE AND WILL HUFF

PAUL E. BIERLEY

THE MUSIC OF HENRY FILLMORE AND WILL HUFF

© 1982 by Paul E. Bierley

INTEGRITY PRESS

10 9 8 7 6 5

Printed in the United States of America

Library of Congress Catalog Card Number 82-81491
ISBN 0-918048-02-8

CONTENTS

INTRODUCTION

This book is intended as a companion to *Hallelujah Trombone !*, the story of the colorful James Henry Fillmore, Jr. (1881-1956).

In the course of his illustrious career as a bandmaster, composer and publisher, Henry Fillmore used his own name and seven pseudonyms. This volume presents a catalog of the music he wrote under all eight names — as well as the music of William L. Huff (1875-1942) of Chillicothe, Ohio.

Why is Huff included? Because Henry Fillmore borrowed the name *Will Huff* for some of his own music.

Several generations of musicians have been under the impression that *Will Huff* was just another of Fillmore's pseudonyms, but nothing could be further from the truth.

It is one of the most amazing coincidences of the music world that the real Will Huff wrote band music and that he, like Henry Fillmore, was a native of Southern Ohio. What's more, he was publishing with a rival Cincinnati music publisher at the time Fillmore unknowingly chose to use the pseudonym *Will Huff*.

By the time Fillmore learned of the existence of the real Will Huff, he had published two marches using the *Huff* pseudonym. He ceased using the name but revived it again twelve years later, and this leads to a fascinating tale.

The intrigue centers around two collections of music published by the Fillmore Brothers Company of Cincinnati. The first was the *Will Huff Band Book* (1913), and the second was the *Huff Par-Excel Band Book* (1916). Each book contained sixteen pieces.

In conversations with friends just before he died, Fillmore revealed that he had written several of the pieces in one or both books. But he declined to identify the pieces. Huff, too, was extremely close-mouthed about the whole affair. It was known for a fact, however, that Fillmore had re-arranged all the pieces by the real Huff (i.e., those pieces published by Fillmore) and had edited them for publishing.

I became aware of the situation while conducting a lengthy study of the copyrights of Fillmore's music at the Library of Congress in Washington, D.C. I was almost finished with the study and had found no clue to the existence of a Will Huff, and I must confess that I was about to disbelieve Fillmore's story that there really was a composer having that name.

Then...a surprise. I found a copyright renewal card for a march called "Salute to Uncle Sam" which read as follows:

Renewed 14 February 1936 by Will Huff
37 Bridge Street, Chillicothe, Ohio

This was quite a shock, because it meant that the mysterious Will Huff had, at least at one time, lived within fifty miles of the part of the country where I had spent most of my life. I had never heard of him. Neither had dozens of musicians I had asked.

I pondered over these circumstances for quite some time. Since Huff had lived in Chillicothe, would any of his relatives still be there? I sat in my studio thinking about this one Sunday afternoon and decided to call the information operator in Chillicothe and ask if there were listings for any Huffs.

"We have a William L. Huff," said the operator.

Will...William L..... That seemed like a good place to start, so I dialed his number.

Yes, this was William L. Huff, he assured me. He listened patiently while I gave a lengthy explanation of the Fillmore-Huff enigma and then asked if he had ever heard of the Will Huff who composed marches and other band music.

"Yes," he replied, "he was my father."

Eureka!

This was just the beginning of my investigations in a completely new area. I found myself doing research on two composers rather than one, and it became fascinating. Three of Huff's children were still living there in Chillicothe: William L., Margerie and Beulah. The following weekend I paid them a visit.

After that first visit with the Huff family, I sought out numerous aging musicians and friends of Will Huff who had been acquainted with him or who had played in one of his bands, not just in Chillicothe but in other parts of Southern Ohio.

Cataloguing Huff's music was difficult indeed. In visiting and corresponding with the Huff family, I was privileged to study such things as handwritten documents and royalty statements on the music which their father had composed for Fillmore.

I then visited with band recording entrepreneur Robert Hoe at his home in Poughkeepsie, New York, and reported on my findings. He had copies of nearly all the *Huff* music, most of which he had painstakingly extracted from the huge stacks of unprocessed music in the bowels of the Library of Congress. He, too, had been mystified over the dual use of the name *Will Huff* and furnished copies of all this music so that I might study it. This proved to be a vital link in my research.

The name *Huff* appeared on the music of four different publishers. Some of the music was not copyrighted, so at first

I was obliged to guess at the dates. Complicating matters was the fact that some of the pieces which bore copyright notices were not actually copyrighted.

Soon it became obvious that the music published by houses other than the Fillmore Brothers Company was composed by Huff himself. But what about those where Henry Fillmore was involved?

I studied the music and what few recordings were available. However, the base of material for comparative study was not broad enough to make an accurate determination. The only answer was to have the unrecorded pieces taped so that I could study them in detail. The next step was to locate a band willing to make the recordings.

Should I approach one of the top military bands, since I knew most of the directors personally? No; there were too many demands for their services as it was. A professional band? Out of the question because of cost. A college band? No — the music was elementary, and the students would find it boring. A community band? None available. That narrowed it down to high school bands.

I was personally acquainted with some ninety high school band directors in this area, but I had my favorite bands and directors. My first choice was the Lincoln High School Band of Gahanna, Ohio, a suburb of Columbus. The director was an old friend, Robert Kessler. Bob's associate at Lincoln High and in the junior high schools was another old friend, James Singer. This would be an ideal situation — Jim and I had been Bob's assistant conductors with the old North American Aviation Concert Band.

This arrangement would have an additional advantage: the school was only a mile from my office, and I could leave for short periods while the recordings were being made. By a stroke of luck, the band rehearsal period coincided with my lunch hour.

I approached Bob with the idea. He talked it over with Jim and the student musicians, and they came up with a brilliant suggestion. Not only would their top band record the pieces, but the theory and harmony class volunteered to study the tapes and music with the intent of unravelling the Fillmore/Huff puzzle. Splendid!

For two weeks, Bob and Jim led the band through the pieces in the *Will Huff Band Book* and the *Huff Par-Excel Band Book*. I brought my tuba each day and played along with the band. Just like old times.

The following weekend I edited the tapes and prepared a study booklet for each member of the theory and harmony class.

By no means was this an ordinary class. It consisted of twelve students from a total of three hundred band and orchestra members and included some of the school's top scholars. Needless to say, I was thrilled and honored by their willingness to undertake such an involved project.

The class listened and re-listened to the tapes, plus other recordings of Huff and Fillmore music, for comparative purposes. The kids were sharp and perceptive and were soon able to distinguish between Huff's style and Fillmore's style.

On the final day of the school year, the verdict was in on all thirty-two pieces in the two *Huff* collections. The score was Huff 26, Fillmore 6. I will take the responsibility for the final judgment and must emphasize the fact that if there were any errors they were honest errors.

This was a big step in my catalog of Henry Fillmore's music. And Will Huff's as well. Armed with these findings, I was able to close the case which might appropriately be called "The Great Will Huff Mystery."

The relationship between Henry Fillmore and the man whose name he inadvertently borrowed will some day be common knowledge. But I shall always have vivid memories of the colossal mixup which once prevailed.

The detailed story of Will Huff and his association with Henry Fillmore is told in my Fillmore biography, *Hallelujah Trombone !* It is my sincere hope that the information presented in these two books will set the record straight once and for all.

Paul E. Bierley

PART ONE

THE MUSIC OF
HENRY FILLMORE

PREFACE TO PART ONE

This section consists of a catalog of the original compositions of Henry Fillmore, plus his arrangements (or direct transcriptions) of the music of other composers.

Fillmore's music, composed under his own name or seven pseudonyms, may be summarized as follows:

Name	Number of Original Compositions	Number of Arrangements of the Works of Others
Henry Fillmore	113	677
Gus Beans	2	-
Harold Bennett	65	-
Ray Hall	3	-
Harry Hartley	6	6
Al Hayes	57	92
Will Huff	8	-
Henrietta Moore	1	-
Totals	255	775

Total Musical Works = 1,030

NUMBERING SYSTEM

In cataloguing Fillmore's *original compositions*, subtitled pieces which are parts of larger works are not counted. For example, *The Christmas Spirit* (cantata) is comprised of fifteen short individual pieces, each having its own title, but the work as a whole is counted as one composition, not fifteen.

The total number of *arrangements (or transcriptions)* includes each individual arrangement which Fillmore made of the works of other composers. If he first arranged a piece for band and then later for orchestra, for example, this counts as two arrangements. Multiple arrangements which he made of his own original music, however, are not counted; this is the preferred way of cataloguing a composer's works.

DATES

The date of each work, appearing in parentheses beside its title, refers to the date of the first copyright, exceptions being cases where copyrights were not obtained. In these cases, the dates of composition or dates of publication are given, if known. It would have been more desirable to have listed the dates of actual composition, but this was not practical because so few of the Fillmore manuscripts have survived.

EDITIONS LISTED

On Fillmore's original compositions, only the first published and other significant editions created by Fillmore himself are listed in this section   More recent editions, edited or arranged by others, are not included.

Quite a few of the Fillmore works were reprinted in collections, such as the *Al Hayes Band Book*, *Famous Fillmore Marches*, etc. These collections are mentioned only where confusion might result if they were not.

DEDICATIONS

Occasionally, Fillmore would dedicate a piece of music to someone or to an institution, event, etc., and the inscription usually would appear on the sheet music just above or below the title. If not printed on all the instrumental parts used by a band or orchestra, the inscription would be found on the part normally used by the conductor — the solo cornet part if for band, or the first violin part if for orchestra. In this book, the dedications are presented word for word as they appear on the music.

NUMBER OF MARCHES

Henry Fillmore ranks with the "march kings" of the world, not because of the quantity of his marches but rather because of the quality of his best ones. The total number of marches he composed was 113. By way of comparison, John Philip Sousa composed 136.

It should be noted, however, that Fillmore wrote only 43 marches under his own name. As a general rule, these were the most difficult ones. The remainder, for bands of beginning or intermediate levels of proficiency, were written under his various pseudonyms.

PUBLISHERS

Of the published works listed in Part One, all were copyrighted and/or published by the Fillmore Brothers Company of Cincinnati, unless otherwise noted. The name Fischer appears often, because Carl Fischer acquired the Fillmore firm in 1951 and continued publication of their catalog. The only other publishers of Henry Fillmore's music were Harry Coleman, the Rudolph Wurlitzer Company and the University of Miami.

COPYRIGHTS

The copyright laws of the United States, recently revised, are now rather complex. The periods of applicability for a copyright or a copyright renewal vary according to the date of first publication of a piece of music (if published). A discussion of all the provisions of copyright law is clearly beyond the scope of this book. However, it should be noted that on some of Fillmore's last works no indication is given herein as to whether or not a copyright has been renewed. This is because the work is still in its original term of copyright and the period during which copyright renewal may be obtained will be later than the publication date of this book.

Only copyrights issued for protection in the United States are listed; the few international copyrights issued are not.

The customary statement of copyright ownership appears on practically every work published by the Fillmore Brothers Company. In several instances, however, works were not actually copyrighted, even though notices appeared. This is surprising, because the Fillmore house kept unusually accurate records. But it is to be expected among publishers which issue great volumes of music. When it is stated in this book that a work was published but not copyrighted, this is usually the explanation.

It should be assumed that copyrights of the works are still active unless the statement "not ren" (copyright not renewed) is given. Further, some unpublished works which were not copyrighted might still be protected, according to existing copyright law.

HAROLD BENNETT COPYRIGHTS

The multitudinous copyrights obtained for the compositions included in the four *Bennett Band Books* resulted in much complication insofar as cataloguing is concerned. The Fillmore house was not consistent in copyrighting these pieces, so the following is offered by way of clarification.

All of the pieces composed under the Harold Bennett pseudonym were first published and copyrighted individually. Later, they were reprinted in collections known as the *Bennet Band Book No. 1, Bennett Band Book No. 2, Bennett Band Book No. 3,* and *Bennett Band Book No. 4.* Books 1 through 3 were all copyrighted on 5 March 1935 (and renewed by Fischer on 12 April 1962). Since the individual pieces had previously been copyrighted, this resulted in double copyright coverages. The *Bennett Band Book No. 4* was not copyrighted as a collection. All copyrights, including the double coverages, are recorded in this book.

The pieces in the *Bennett Band Book No. 1* and the *Bennett Band Book No. 2* were also published in orchestra editions as the *Bennett Orchestra Folio No. 1* and the *Bennett Orchestra Folio No. 2,* respectively. Strangely, these orchestra collections were not copyrighted.

To avoid confusion in listing the Bennett pieces, it is noted herein if they are included in any of the band books or orchestra folios.

LEGEND FOR PART ONE

Band	For band
BBB#1	Included in the *Bennett Band Book No. 1*
BBB#2	Included in the *Bennett Band Book No. 2*
BBB#3	Included in the *Bennett Band Book No. 3*
BBB#4	Included in the *Bennett Band Book No. 4*
BOF#1	Included in the *Bennett Orchestra Folio No. 1*
BOF#2	Included in the *Bennett Orchestra Folio No. 2*
Coleman	Harry Coleman, Philadelphia, Pennsylvania
©	Copyright, or copyrighted
Fischer	Carl Fischer, New York, New York
HPEBB	Included in the *Huff Par-Excel Band Book*
HPEOF	Included in the *Huff Par-Excel Orchestra Folio*
Orch	For orchestra
Publ	Publisher, or published
Ren	Renewal of copyright, or renewed
U of M	University of Miami, Coral Gables, Florida
Wurlitzer	Rudolph Wurlitzer Company, Cincinnati, Ohio

MUSIC COMPOSED UNDER THE NAME HENRY FILLMORE

"All Day" - march (1922)
   (Based on themes of Suppe's overture, "Morning, Noon and
   Night in Vienna")
   ⓒ: Band, 5 Jun 1922; ren 30 Jun 1949.

"Americans We" - march (1929)
   "To all of us"
   ⓒ: Band, 11 Mar 1929; ren Fischer 19 Apr 1956
      Orch, same.

"Better Be Good" - children's song (1908)
   Words by Lizzie DeArmond
   ⓒ: Vocal and piano, 14 Oct 1908; ren 3 Aug 1936.

"The Big Brass Band" [see "King Karl King"]

"Bones Trombone" - smear (1922)
   ⓒ: Band, 14 Mar 1922; ren 30 Jun 1949.
      Also publ for orch but not ⓒ.
      Also publ for trombone and piano but not ⓒ.

"Boss Trombone" - smear (1929)
   ⓒ: Band, 17 Aug 1929; ren Fischer 24 Aug 1956.
      Orch, same.
      Trombone and piano, same.

"Bull Bull Bulldogs" - pep song (ca. 1947)
   Words by Henry Fillmore
   Not ⓒ or publ. Vocal and band.

"Bull Trombone" - smear (1924)
   ⓒ: Band, 5 May 1924; ren Henry Fillmore 24 Mar 1952.
      Orch, 19 May 1924; not ren.
      Trombone and piano, 9 Jun 1924; ren Henry Fillmore
         8 Apr 1952.

"Celtic" - romance (1933)
   Not ⓒ or publ. Band.

"Chasing the Fox" - novelty (1929)
   Not ⓒ or publ. Band.

"Chasing a Pig"("Mike at the Hog Calling Contest") - novelty
   (1929)
   Based on a traditional Irish tune
   Not ⓒ or publ. Band.

"The Chimes of Iron Mountain" - chimes solo (1955)
   "To the folks of Lake Wales, Florida, the home of the Bok
      Tower"
   ⓒ: Chimes and band, Fischer 2 Aug 1955.

"The Cincinnati Zoo" [see "Americans We"]

"Christmas Dollies" - motion song for children (1912)
   Words by Eleanor Allen Schroll
   ⓒ: Vocal and piano, 23 Oct 1912; ren 16 Sep 1940.

The Christmas Spirit - Christmas cantata/playlet for children (1914)
  Libretto by Julia E. Burnand
  Pieces: "Overture," "The Festal Day Is Near," "Spirit's Song," "Santa Claus Will Soon Be Here," "O Yes, We've Had Enough," "Come Out O Come Out," "Long Long Ago," "We Greet You," "Christmas Will Last All the Year," "A Song of Cheer," "Softly O'er Judea's Hills," "Jolly Old Santa Claus," "Santa's Arrival," "'Tis Merry, Merry Christmas," and "Closing Chorus."
  ©: Vocal and piano, 7 Nov 1914; ren 2 Jly 1942.
     "Overture," [only] piano, 18 Nov 1914; ren 2 Jly 1942.

"The Circus Bee" - march (1908)
  ©: Band, 28 Feb 1908; ren 17 Feb 1936.

"Comin' Round the Mountain" - humoresque (1934)
  ©: Band, 5 Sep 1934; ren Fischer 21 Sep 1961.

"The Contest" ("Who Wins?") ("Mike and the Children") - novelty (1928)
  Incorporating several popular tunes
  Not © or publ. Band.

"The Crosley March" (1928)
  "To Powell Crosley, Jr., President, the Crosley Radio Corporation, Cincinnati, Ohio."
  ©: Band, 31 Mar 1928; ren Fischer 11 May 1955.
     Orch, same.

Crowned with Light - Easter cantata for children (1922)
  Lyrics and recitations by Eleanor Allen Schroll
  Pieces: "Crowned with Light," "Glory and Bloom," "Angels Wait in the Garden," "Joy in the Air," "Christ Is Risen from the Dead," "Waking Up," "Tell Me the Easter Story," "Lift Up Your Hearts," "The Open Gate," and "Jesus Goes Before You to Galilee."
  ©: Vocal and piano, 11 Feb 1922; not ren.

"The Cuckoo" - march humoresque (1912)
  ©: Orch, 8 Apr 1912; ren 1 Nov 1939.
     Piano, 15 Apr 1912; not ren.
     Band, 14 May 1912; ren 1 Nov 1939.

"Deep Bass" - tuba solo (1927)
  ©: Tuba and band, 4 Nov 1927; ren Fischer 1 Dec 1954.
     Also publ for tuba and piano but not ©.

"The Dog and the Music Box" - novelty (1929)
  Not © or publ. Band.

"Dusty Trombone" - smear (1923)
  ©: Band, 19 Mar 1923; ren 28 Feb 1951.
     Orch, 19 Mar 1923; ren 14 Jly 1950.

Also publ for trombone and piano but not ©.

"An Earl" - solo for trombone, baritone horn, cornet or sax-
   ophone (1928)
   "To Earl Miller, trombone soloist, The Fillmore Band"
   © : Solo instrument and band, 31 Mar 1928; ren Fischer
         14 Apr 1955.
         Solo instrument and orch, 28 Apr 1928; ren Fischer
         8 Aug 1955.

Easter Bells - Easter cantata for children (1913)
   Lyrics and recitations by Eleanor Allen Schroll
   Pieces: "Ring the Happy Easter Bells," "Christ the Lord,
         Is Risen," "Lo! The Easter Dawn," "Clap and Sing,"
         "Beautiful Lilies," "His Love Untold," "O Joyful
         Morn," and "Sing All Ye People."
   © : Vocal and piano, 10 Feb 1913; not ren.
Easter Joy-Bells - Easter cantata for children (1912)
   Lyrics by Palmer Hartsough; recitations by Palmer Hart-
         sough, Lizzie DeArmond, Margaret E. Sangster and Mrs.
         R.N. Turner
   Pieces: "Easter Marching Song," "O Bells of Easter,"
         "This Is Easter Day," "Hail the Victor!;" "Sing
         Pretty Birdies," "Love for Me," "There's a Gentle
         Voice," "Bright Flowers of Easter," "Lilies of
         Easter," and "Blessed Morn Triumphant."
             Note: "Easter Marching Song" was reprinted as a
                     hymn, "With Steady Step," with one addi-
                     tional verse, also by Palmer Hartsough,
                     in the collection *Songs of Praise* (1912).
                     "Oh Bells of Easter" was reprinted as a
                     hymn under three different names. First,
                     as "Hallelujah! Hallelujah!," with new
                     verses by Palmer Hartsough, in the collec-
                     tion *Songs of Praise* (1912). Second, as
                     "When Lord's Day Morning Comes," with the
                     same verses as "Hallelujah! Hallelujah!,"
                     in the collection *Hymns for Today* (1920).
                     Third, as "O Lord of Hosts," with new ver-
                     ses by Eleanor Allen Schroll, in *A Hymnal
                     for Joyous Youth* (1927). "Hail the Vic-
                     tor" was reprinted five times as a hymn,
                     "Hear the Trumpet Call," with new verses
                     by Palmer Hartsough. First, in the col-
                     lection *Songs of Praise* (1912). Second, in
                     the collection *Quartets and Choruses for
                     Men* (1913). Third, as separate sheet mu-
                     sic for male quartet (1913). Fourth, in
                     the collection *Hymns for Today* (1920).
                     Fifth, in *A Hymnal for Joyous Youth* (1927).
                     "Love for Me" was reprinted twice as a
                     hymn, with one additional verse, also by
                     Palmer Hartsough. First, in the collec-

tion *Songs of Praise* (1912). Second, in *A Hymnal for Joyous Youth* (1927). "Lilies of Easter" was reprinted as a hymn, "He's My Friend," with new verses, also by Palmer Hartsough, in the collection *Songs of Praise* (1912).

ⓒ: Vocal and piano, 10 Feb 1912; not ren.
"Hear the Trumpet Call," [only] male quartet, not ⓒ.
"O Lord of Hosts," [only] vocal and piano, 29 Apr 1927; ren Henry Fillmore 30 Dec 1954.

"Five Ways to Play America Exultant March" - humoresque (ca. 1934)
Five variations on "America Exultant" march, by Al Hayes Not ⓒ or publ. Band.

"The Footlifter" - march ("Penny-a-Day March") (1935)
"To Harry T. Garner, Secretary of the Cincinnati Automobile Dealers Association."
ⓒ: Band, 25 Oct 1935; ren Fischer 7 Dec 1962.

"Gifted Leadership" - march (1927)
"To Frank Simon, Director of Armco Band, Middletown, Ohio"
ⓒ: Band, 11 Jun 1927; ren Fischer 2 Aug 1954.
Orch, 3 Aug 1927; ren Fischer 28 Oct 1954.

"Giving Mike the Ha Ha" - novelty (1930)
Not ⓒ or publ. Band.

"Glory to God on High" - song (1913)
Words by Palmer Hartsough
ⓒ: Vocal and piano, 22 Oct 1913; ren 27 Mar 1941.

"Go Raiders Go" - pep song (1946)
Words by Henry Fillmore
"To Fred McCall - Bandmaster, Edison Hi, Miami, Florida"
ⓒ: Vocal and band, 9 Nov 1946; ren Fischer 9 Jan 1974.

"Golden Friendships" - march (1926)
"To the members of Syrian Temple Shrine Band, Cincinnati, Ohio"
ⓒ: Band, 2 Jun 1926; ren Henry Fillmore 9 Sep 1953.
Orch, 14 Oct 1926; ren Henry Fillmore 19 Oct 1953.

"Ha Ha Ha" - novelty (1933)
ⓒ: Band, 6 Sep 1933; ren Fischer 15 Sep 1960.

"Hail! Hail to Edison" - pep march (1946)
ⓒ: Band, 9 Nov 1946; ren Fischer 9 Jan 1974.

Hail! Joyful Morning! - Easter cantata for children (1912)
Lyrics and recitations by Lizzie DeArmond
Pieces: "Hail! Joyful Morning!," "Joy for the Day," "The Wonderful Cross," "Loving Promises," "Chime On

Sweet Bells of Easter," "Praises Sing," "Tell the News," "Let the Whole World Ring," "Easter Lilies," "Wake Up Pretty World," "Hail the King of Glory," "Meditation," "Give to King Jesus," and "Worship the Lord Most Glorious."
   ⓒ: Vocal and piano, 19 Feb 1912; not ren.

"Hallelujah! Hallelujah!" [see *Easter Joy-Bells*]

"Hallelujah Trombone" [see "Shoutin' Liza Trombone]

"Ham Trombone" - smear (1929)
   ⓒ: Band, 17 Aug 1929; ren Fischer 24 Aug 1956.
      Orch, same.
      Trombone and piano, same.

Happy Children's Day - Children's Day cantata (1913)
   Lyrics and recitations by Eleanor Allen Schroll
   Pieces: "Come Rejoicing," "Joy Everywhere," "Gifts from Above," "Earth in Beauty Glowing," "Children's Day Has Come," "Blessings Sweet Blessings," "Give," "Jesus Needs Us," "June Fair June," and "Eternal Praise."
   ⓒ: Vocal and piano, 10 May 1913; not ren.

"Hear the Trumpet Call" [see *Easter Joy-Bells*]

Henry Fillmore's Jazz Trombonist (1919)
   Collection of exercises and examples, with brief instructions
   ⓒ: Trombone, 27 Feb 1919; ren 6 Oct 1946.

"He's My Friend" [see *Easter Joy-Bells*]

"The Hikers" - patrol (1933)
   Not ⓒ or publ. Band.

"His Excellency" - march (1909)
   ⓒ: Band, 28 Jun 1909; not ren.
      Orch, same.

"His Honor" - march (1934)
   "To the Honorable Russell Wilson, Mayor of Cincinnati"
   ⓒ: Band, 22 Jan 1934; ren Fischer 4 May 1961.
      Orch, 14 Sep 1934; not ren.

"Honor and Glory" - march (1905)
   ⓒ: Band, 15 Jun 1905; ren 17 May 1933.

"Hot Trombone" - smear (1921)
   ⓒ: Band, 1 Feb 1921, again 14 Apr 1921; not ren.
      Orch, 1 Feb 1921; not ren.
      Also publ for trombone and piano but not ⓒ.

"How Do You Do!" - motion song for children (1911)
   Words by Jessie Brown Pounds
   In collection, *Happy Songs for Happy Children*, not ⓒ.

"I Have Found the Fount of Gladness" - hymn (1913)
   Words by Palmer Hartsough
   ©: Male voices, in collection, *Quartets and Choruses for Men*, 15 Dec 1913; ren Henry Fillmore 27 Mar 1951.

"In Uniform" - march (1905)
   ©: Band, Coleman 20 May 1905; not ren.

"Jackson Pep" - pep song (1945)
   Words by Henry Fillmore
   Not © or publ. Band.

Jazz Trombonist [see *Henry Fillmore's Jazz Trombonist*]

"Join All to Sing" [see *Life and Glory*]

"King Karl King" - march ("The Big Brass Band," or "The Three B's") (1959)
   ©: Band, Fischer 24 Sep 1959.

"The Kingdom of the Lord" - hymn (1913)
   Words by Palmer Hartsough
   ©: Male voices, in collection, *Quartets and Choruses for Men*, 15 Dec 1913; ren Henry Fillmore 27 Mar 1951.

"The Klaxon" - march ("March of the Automobiles") (1930)
   "To the producers of the klaxon automobile horn"
   ©: Band, 19 Jul 1930; ren Fischer 1 Aug 1957.

"Lassus Trombone" - smear (1915)
   ©: Band, 14 Jun 1915; ren 5 Apr 1943.
       Orch, same.
       Trombone and piano, 16 Aug 1919; not ren.

Life and Glory - Easter cantata (1917)
   Lyrics and recitations by Eleanor Allen Schroll
   Pieces: "Joy Joy Joy," "Open Wide the Gates," "He Is Risen," "Join All to Sing," "Sing a Song of Easter," "He Lives," "Spring Is Here," "He Will Roll the Stone Away," "Dawn of Glory," and "Tell the Easter Story."
           Note: "Join All to Sing" was reprinted as a hymn in the collection *Hymns for Today* (1920). "Dawn of Glory" was reprinted as a hymn with new verses, also by Eleanor Allen Schroll, in *A Hymnal for Joyous Youth* (1927). "Tell the Easter Story" was reprinted twice as a hymn, "Tell the "Gospel Story," with new verses, also by Eleanor Allen Schroll. First, in *A Hymnal for Joyous Youth* (1927). Second, in *The New Praise Hymnal* (1927).
   ©: Vocal and piano, 27 Feb 1917; not ren.
       "Tell the Gospel Story," [only] vocal and piano, 29 Apr 1927; ren Henry Fillmore 30 Dec 1954.

"Lightning Fingers" - clarinet solo (1930)
  "To Luise Reszke, the Phantom Clarinetist"
  ©: Clarinet and band, 19 Jly 1930; ren Fischer 1 Aug
      1957.
      Also publ for clarinet and piano but not ©.

"Lord Baltimore" - march (1904)
  ©: Band, 18 Apr 1904; ren 30 Jan 1932.
      Orch, same.

"Love for Me" [see *Easter Joy-Bells*]

"A Loyal Gideon Band" - hymn (1913)
  Words by Frona L. Scott
  ©: Male voices, in collection, *Quartets and Choruses
      for Men*, 15 Dec 1913; ren Henry Fillmore, 27 Mar
      1951.

"Lucky Trombone" - smear (1926)
  ©: Band, 2 Jun 1926; ren Henry Fillmore 2 Oct 1953.
      Orch, 14 Oct 1926; ren Henry Fillmore 19 Oct 1953.
      Also publ for trombone and piano but not ©.

"The Man Among Men" - march (1923)
  "To William J. Howard, Past Potentate, Syrian Temple"
  ©: Band, 19 Mar 1923; ren 28 Feb 1951.
      Orch, 19 Apr 1923; not ren.

"The Man of the Hour" - march (1924)
  "To the Honorable Charles P. Taft, General Chairman, Cin-
      cinnati New Masonic Temple Campaign Committee"
  ©: Band, 5 May 1924, again 19 May 1924; ren Henry Fill-
      more 24 Mar 1952.

"March of the Automobiles" [see "The Klaxon"]

"March of the Waves" [see "Waves"]

"The Marvel" - march (1906)
  ©: Band, 22 Aug 1906; ren 3 Aug 1934.
      Orch, same.

"Men of Florida" - march ("We're Men of Florida") (1949)
  Words by Henry Fillmore
  ©: Band, 28 Oct 1949; ren Fischer 24 Feb 1977.

"Men of Ohio" - march (1921)
  "To the President, Warren G. Harding, and his staunch loy-
      alists"
  ©: Band, 28 Apr 1921; ren 13 May 1948.
      Orch, 2 May 1921; ren 13 May 1948.

"Miami" - march (1938)
  "To the folks of Greater Miami, Florida"
  ©: Band, 30 Nov 1938; ren Fischer, 24 Feb 1966.

"Miami U-How-Dee-Doo" - pep song (1950)
  Words by Henry Fillmore
  "To Coach Andy Gustafson"

© : Vocal and band, U of M 10 Nov 1950; not ren.

"Mike and the Children" [see "The Contest"]

"Mike at the Hog Calling Contest" [see "Chasing a Pig"]

"Mike Hunting Birds" - novelty (1929)
Not © or publ. Band.

"Military Escort in 5 Ways" ("Toying with Military Escort")
- humoresque (1930)
Variations on "Military Escort" - march by Harold Bennett
© : Band, 19 Jly 1930; ren Fischer 1 Aug 1957.

"Miss Trombone" - smear (1908)
© : Band, 29 Aug 1908; ren 3 Aug 1936.
Orch, same.
Also publ for trombone and piano but not © .

"More Fraternity" - march (1916)
"To the International Convention of the A.F.of M., Cincinnati, May 8-13, 1916, compliments of the Musical Messenger"
© : Band, 10 May 1916; ren 8 Nov 1943.
Orch, same.

"Mose Trombone" - smear (1919)
"To John Klohr"
© : Band, 20 Feb 1919; ren 6 Oct 1946.
Orch, same.
Also publ for trombone and piano but not © .

"My Master Was a Worker" - hymn (1920)
Words by William George Tarrant
© : Vocal and piano, in collection, *Hymns for Today*, 1
May 1920; ren 21 Jly 1947.

"The National Press Club" - march (1932)
"To the officers and members of the National Press Club,
Washington, D.C."
© : Band, 18 Aug 1932; ren Fischer 17 Sep 1959.

"Noble Men" - march (1922)
"To Ralph Tingle, Potentate, Syrian Temple, and members,
A.A.O.N.M.S."
© : Band, 15 Apr 1922; ren 30 Jun 1949.
Orch, 1 May 1922; ren 30 Jun 1949.

"North-South College All Stars" - march (1953)
"To the Mahi Shrine Annual Charity Football Classic,
Christmas Night, Miami, Florida"
© : Band, 10 Mar 1953.

"O Lord of Hosts" [see *Easter Joy-Bells*]

"O Praise Him for the Morning" [see *The Star-Lit Way*]

"O Santa Please Come Down My Chimney" - children's song
(1910)

Words by Elizabeth F. Guptill
ⓒ: Vocal and piano, 24 Oct 1910; not ren.

"O You Christmas Candy!" - motion song for children (1912)
Words by Eleanor Allen Schroll
ⓒ: Vocal and piano, 26 Oct 1912; ren 16 Sep 1940.

"Of All Lofty Praises" [see *Life and Glory*]

"An Old Time Political Parade" - novelty march (1929)
ⓒ: Band, 13 Apr 1929; not ren.
   Orch, 13 Apr 1929; ren Fischer 16 Jly 1956.

"On the Wings of the Wind" - intermezzo two-step (1907)
ⓒ: Band, 20 Apr 1907; not ren.
   Orch, same.

"Orange Bowl" - march (1939)
ⓒ: Band, 22 Nov 1939; ren Fischer 10 Jan 1967.
   Orch, 22 Dec 1939; not ren.

"Our Happy Land" - hymn (1913)
Words by Adaline H. Beery
ⓒ: Male voices, in collection, *Quartets and Choruses for Men*, 15 Dec 1913; ren Henry Fillmore 27 Mar 1951.

"Our Own Red, White and Blue" - song (1917)
Words by Eleanor Allen Schroll
ⓒ: Vocal and piano, 23 Apr 1917; ren 2 Dec 1944.
   Band, 11 Jun 1917; ren 15 Apr 1945.
   Orch, same as band.

"Over the Waves" [see "Waves"]

"Pahson Trombone" - smear (1916)
ⓒ: Band, 29 Mar 1916; ren 8 Nov 1943.
   Orch, same.
   Trombone and piano, 14 May 1918; ren 30 Nov 1945.

"Paths of Pleasantness and Peace" - hymn (1927)
Words by Eleanor Allen Schroll
ⓒ: Vocal and piano, in collection, *A Hymnal for Joyous Youth*, 29 Apr 1927; not ren.

"Penny-a-Day March" [see "The Footlifter"]

"The Phantom" - clarinet solo (1928)
"To Luise Reszke"
Not ⓒ or publ. Clarinet and band.

"Playfellow" - march (1927)
"To a dog. Our dog, Mike. A faithful, playful hound."
ⓒ: Band, 12 May 1927; ren Fischer 2 Aug 1954.
   Orch, 4 Nov 1927; ren Fischer 1 Dec 1954.

"The Poet, Peasant and Light Cavalryman" - march (1915)
Based on Franz von Suppe's overtures
ⓒ: Band, 11 Jan 1915; ren 2 Jly 1942.
   Orch, 20 Jan 1915; ren 23 Oct 1942.

16

"The Presidents March" (1956)
 "Dedicated to the Presidents of the University of Miami,
  Coral Gables, Florida."
 ©: Band, Fischer 3 Apr 1956.

"Pure Food and Health" [see "Americans We"]

"Ring Out the Old Ring In the New" - hymn (1920)
 Words from the poem by Alfred Tennyson
 ©: Vocal and piano, in collection, *Hymns for Today*,
    1 May 1920; ren 21 Jly 1947.

"Rolling Thunder" - march (1916)
 "To Ed Hicker"
 ©: Band, 24 Mar 1916; ren 8 Nov 1943.

"Roses" - song (1928)
 Based on a poem from the play *Rollo's Wild Oats* by Clare
  Beecher Kummer
 Not © or publ. Vocal and piano.

"Safe in the Arms of Jesus" - medley march (ca. 1906)
 Based on the hymns "Safe in the Arms of Jesus" and "Who-
  soever Will May Come"
 Not ©. Band.

"St. Edmund" - march (1907)
 Incorporating the hymn tune "St. Edmund" by Arthur Sulli-
  van.
 ©: Band, 20 Apr 1907; not ren.
    Orch, same.

"Sally Trombone" - smear (1917)
 ©: Band, 13 Jan 1917; ren 2 Dec 1944.
    Orch, same.
    Trombone and piano, 14 May 1918; ren 30 Nov 1945.
    Piano, 16 Aug 1919; not ren.

"Sea Hawks" - pep song (1946)
 Words by Henry Fillmore
 ©: Vocal and band, 29 Nov 1946; ren Fischer 14 Jan 1974.

"Shall We Gather at the River" - medley march (1906)
 Based on the hymns "Shall We Gather at the River" and
  "Home Over There"
 ©: Band, 22 Aug 1906; ren 3 Aug 1934.

"Shoutin' Liza Trombone" - smear (first edition was "Hallelujah Trombone") (1920)
 ©: Band (as "Hallelujah Trombone"), 7 Feb 1920; not ren.
    Orch (as "Hallelujah Trombone"), same.
    Band (as "Shoutin' Liza Trombone"), 2 Mar 1920; ren
     21 Jly 1947.
    Orch (as "Shoutin' Liza Trombone"), same.
    Trombone and piano (as "Shoutin' Liza Trombone"),
     same.
    Piano (as "Shoutin' Liza Trombone"), 17 Apr 1920;
     not ren.

"Slim Trombone" - smear (1918)
    ⓒ: Band, 15 Apr 1918; ren 30 Nov 1945.
        Orch, same.
        Trombone and piano, same.
        Piano, 18 Aug 1919; not ren.

"Spirit Divine" - hymn (1913)
    Words by Palmer Hartsough
    ⓒ: Male voices, in collection, *Quartets and Choruses
        for Men*, 15 Dec 1913; ren Henry Fillmore 27 Mar
        1951.

The Star-Lit Way - Christmas cantata (1913)
    Lyrics by Palmer Hartsough and Eleanor Allen Schroll;
        recitations by Elizabeth F. Guptill, Mrs. J.M. Hunter,
        Mabel J. Rosemon, Grace Schoettler and Edyth M. Worm-
        wood
    Pieces: "Christmas Greeting," "The Star-Lit Way," "Merry
        Christmas We Bring," "Sweet Thoughts of Grati-
        tude," "Start the Joy-Bells Ringing," "Wonderful
        Love," "Christmas Bells," "Feed God's Poor," "My
        Savior," "Come to the Lowly Manger," and "Closing
        Song."
            Note: "Christmas Greeting" was reprinted as a
                hymn, "O Praise Him for the Morning,"
                with new verses by Eleanor Allen Schroll,
                in *A Hymnal for Joyous Youth* (1927).
                "Sweet Thoughts of Gratitude" was reprint-
                ed as a hymn, "Sweet Are the Songs of the
                Wild Birds," with the same verses, in the
                collection *Hymns for Today* (1920).
    ⓒ: Vocal and piano, 29 Oct 1913; not ren.

"Sugar" - humoresque (no date)
    Not ⓒ or publ. Band.

"The Sunbeams Shining Brightly" - hymn (1920)
    Words by Mary Brainard Smith
    ⓒ: Vocal and piano, in collection, *Hymns for Today*,
        1 May 1920; ren 21 Jly 1947.

"Sweet Are the Songs of the Wild Birds" [see *The Star-Lit
    Way*]

"Teddy Trombone" - smear (1911)
    "To Teddy Hahn"
    ⓒ: Band, 6 Mar 1911; ren 28 Jan 1939.
        Orch, same.
        Trombone and piano, 14 May 1918; ren 30 Nov 1945.

"Tell the Gospel Story" [see *Life and Glory*]

"Tell Mother I'll Be There" - medley march (1905)
    Based on the song, "Tell Mother I'll Be There," by Char-
    les M. Fillmore
    ⓒ: Band, 1 May 1905; ren 10 May 1933.
        Orch, same.

"The Three B's" [see "King Karl King"]

"Tosti's Goodbye March" (1922)
Based on the song "Good-bye" by F. Paolo Tosti
© : Band, 26 Apr 1922; ren 30 Jun 1949.

"Toying with Military Escort" [see "Military Escort in 5 Ways"]

"Traffic" [see "Watch the Traffic Lights"]

"Troopers Tribunal" - march (1905)
© : Band, 15 Jun 1905; ren 17 May 1933.

"The Trumpet Call of God" - hymn (1913)
Words by Palmer Hartsough
© : Male voices, in collection, *Quartets and Choruses for Men*, 15 Dec 1913; ren Henry Fillmore 27 Mar 1951.

"The U.S.of A. Armed Forces" - march (1942)
© : Band, 2 Oct 1942; not ren.

"Vashti" - march (1904)
© : Piano, 25 Jan 1904; ren 14 Jan 1932.
Band, 18 Apr 1904; ren 30 Jan 1932.
Orch, same as band.

"The Victorious First" - march (1907)
"Respectfully dedicated to the 1st Regt. O.N.G."
© : Band, Coleman 31 Mar 1907; not ren.
Note: Published by Fischer; Coleman obtained ©
before Fischer acquired the Coleman catalog
in 1907.

"Watch the Traffic Lights" - humoresque ("Traffic") (1930)
Narrated, interspersed with fragments of numerous popular tunes.
Not © or publ. Band.

"Waves" - march ("March of the Waves") (1943)
Based on the waltz, "Sobre las Olas," or "Over the Waves"
© : Band, 5 Mar 1943; not ren.

"We Will Be True" - hymn (1913)
Words by Palmer Hartsough
© : Male voices, in collection, *Quartets and Choruses for Men*, 15 Dec 1913; ren Henry Fillmore 27 Mar 1951.

"We're Men of Florida" [see "Men of Florida"]

"When Lord's Day Morning Comes" [see *Easter Joy-Bells*]

"When Our Dear Old Santa Comes" - children's song (1913)
Words by Palmer Hartsough
© : Vocal and piano, 22 Oct 1913; ren Henry Fillmore 27 Mar 1941.

"Whistling Farmer Boy" - novelty (1925)
© : Band, 6 Feb 1925; ren Henry Fillmore 7 Mar 1952.

Orch, 28 Feb 1925; ren Henry Fillmore 14 May 1952.

"Who Wins?" [see "The Contest"]

"The Wireless S.O.S." - hymn (1913)
　　Words by Palmer Hartsough
　　ⓒ: Male voices, in collection, *Quartets and Choruses for Men*, 15 Dec 1913; ren Henry Fillmore 27 Mar 1951.

"With Steady Step" [see *Easter Joy-Bells*]

"136th U.S.A. Field Artillery" - march (1918)
　　"To Colonel Paul L. Mitchell, Commanding"
　　ⓒ: Band, 5 Jly 1918; ren 30 Nov 1945.
　　　　Orch, same.
　　　　Piano, 3 Dec 1918, again 15 Mar 1919; not ren.

MUSIC COMPOSED BY HENRY FILLMORE
UNDER THE PSEUDONYM GUS BEANS

"Mt. Healthy" - march (1916)
　　ⓒ: Band, 29 Jan 1916; ren 8 Nov 1943.
　　　　Orch, same.

"Nut Stuff" - humoresque (no date)
　　Narrated, interspersed with fragments of numerous popular tunes.
　　Not ⓒ or publ. Band.

MUSIC COMPOSED BY HENRY FILLMORE
UNDER THE PSEUDONYM HAROLD BENNETT

"Activity" - march (1923)
　　ⓒ: Band, 15 Jan 1923, again 5 Mar 1935; ren 14 Jly 1950, again Fischer 12 Apr 1962.
　　　　Orch, 10 Nov 1923; ren 28 Feb 1951.
　　　　BBB#1, BOF#1.

"Advance" - march (1912)
　　ⓒ: Band, 5 Feb 1912, again 5 Mar 1935; ren 1 Nov 1939, again Fischer 12 Apr 1962.
　　　　Orch, 5 Feb 1912; ren 1 Nov 1939.
　　　　BBB#3.

"Al and Hal" - duet for cornet and trombone (1937)
　　ⓒ: Band, 16 Aug 1937; ren Fischer 3 Sep 1964.
　　　　BBB#4.

"Aline" - march (1937)
　　ⓒ: Band, 17 May 1937; ren Fischer 24 Jly 1964.
　　　　BBB#4.

"Ambition" - overture (1923)

Ⓒ: Band, 15 Jan 1923, again 5 Mar 1935; ren 14 Jly 1950,
    again Fischer 12 Apr 1962.
    Orch, 10 Nov 1923; ren 28 Feb 1951.
    BBB#1, BOF#1.

"Annette" - waltz (1918)
    Ⓒ: Band, 5 Jly 1918, again 5 Mar 1935; ren 30 Nov 1945,
        again Fischer 12 Apr 1962.
        Orch, 3 Oct 1931; not ren.
        BBB#3.

"Anona" - serenade (1926)
    Ⓒ: Band, 17 Apr 1926, again 5 Mar 1935; ren Fischer 28
        Jly 1953, again Fischer 12 Apr 1962.
        Orch, 14 Oct 1926; ren Fischer 19 Oct 1953.
        BBB#2, BOF#2.

"At Sight" - march (1928)
    Ⓒ: Band, 16 Jly 1928, again 5 Mar 1935; ren Fischer 12
        Apr 1962.
        Orch, 3 Oct 1931; not ren.
        BBB#3.

"Aunt Hannah" - characteristic march and two-step (1926)
    Ⓒ: Band, 17 Mar 1926, again 5 Mar 1935; ren Fischer 28
        Jly 1953, again Fischer 12 Apr 1962.
        Orch, 12 Oct 1926; ren Fischer 19 Oct 1953.
        BBB#2, BOF#2.

"Biga" - march (1937)
    Ⓒ: Band, 16 Aug 1937; ren Fischer 3 Sep 1964.
        BBB#4.

"Bliss Eternal" - waltz (1917)
    Ⓒ: Band, 1 May 1917; ren 2 Dec 1944.
        Orch, same.

"Bright Star" - overture (1921)
    Ⓒ: Band, 5 Jan 1921, again 5 Mar 1935; ren Fischer 5 Apr
        1962.
        Orch, 17 Jan 1921; not ren.
        BBB#3.

"The Buglers" - overture (1926)
    Ⓒ: Band, 16 Mar 1926, again 5 Mar 1935; ren Fischer 28
        Jly 1953, again Fischer 12 Apr 1962.
        Orch, 14 Oct 1926; ren Fischer 19 Oct 1953.
        BBB#2, BOF#2.

"Chalma" - waltz (1923)
    Ⓒ: Band, 27 Jan 1923, again 5 Mar 1935, ren 14 Jly 1950,
        again Fischer 12 Apr 1962.
        Orch, 10 Nov 1923; ren 28 Feb 1951.
        BBB#1, BOF#1.

"Chimes of Love" [see "Village Chimes"]

"College Boy" - march (1926)

      Ⓒ : Band, 17 Mar 1926, again 5 Mar 1935; ren Fischer 28
          Jly 1953, again Fischer 12 Apr 1962.
         Orch, 14 Oct 1926; ren Fischer 19 Oct 1953.
         BBB#2, BOF#2.

"Concord" - march (1926)
    Ⓒ : Band, 17 Mar 1926, again 5 Mar 1935; ren Fischer 28
         Jly 1953, again Fischer 12 Apr 1962.
       Orch, 14 Oct 1926; ren Fischer 19 Oct 1953.
       BBB#2, BOF#2.

"Courage" - march (1919)
    Ⓒ : Band, 5 Jun 1919, again 5 Aug 1919, again 5 Mar 1935;
         ren 6 Oct 1946, again Fischer 12 Apr 1962.
       Orch, 20 Oct 1931; not ren.
       BBB#3.

"Dawn" - reverie (1926)
    Ⓒ : Band, 17 Mar 1926, again 5 Mar 1935; ren Fischer 28
         Jly 1953, again Fischer 12 Apr 1962.
       Orch, 14 Oct 1926; ren Fischer 19 Oct 1953.
       BBB#2, BOF#2.

"Delmar" - march (1926)
    Ⓒ : Band, 17 Mar 1926, again 5 Mar 1935; ren Fischer 28
         Jly 1953, again Fischer 12 Apr 1962.
       Orch, 14 Oct 1926; ren Fischer 19 Oct 1953.
       BBB#2, BOF#2.

"Dōn A Do Dat" - fox trot (1931)
    Ⓒ : Band, 19 Feb 1931, again 5 Mar 1935; ren Fischer 20
         Mar 1958, again Fischer 12 Apr 1962.
       Orch, 20 Oct 1931; not ren.
       BBB#3.

"Eels" - a trombone "zipper" (1937)
    Ⓒ : Band, 16 Aug 1937; ren Fischer 3 Sep 1964.
       BBB#4.

"Energy" - overture (1926)
    Ⓒ : Band, 17 Mar 1926, again 5 Mar 1935; ren Fischer 28
         Jly 1953, again Fischer 12 Apr 1962.
       Orch, 14 Oct 1926; ren Fischer 19 Oct 1953.
       BBB#2, BOF#2.

"Genius" - march (1937)
    Ⓒ : Band, 16 Aug 1937; ren Fischer 3 Sep 1964.
       BBB#4.

"Gyral" - fast dance (1937)
    Ⓒ : Band, 16 Aug 1937; ren Fischer 3 Sep 1964.
       BBB#4.

"Havana" - Cuban serenade (1931)
    Ⓒ : Band, 19 Feb 1931, again 5 Mar 1935; ren Fischer 12
         Apr 1962.
       Orch, 3 Oct 1931; not ren.
       BBB#3.

"Have a Little Fun" - novelty (1926)
    ©: Band, 17 Mar 1926, again 5 Mar 1935; ren Fischer 28
        Jly 1953, again Fischer 12 Apr 1962.
        Orch, 14 Oct 1926; ren Fischer 19 Oct 1953.
        BBB#2, BOF#2.

"Headway" - march (1920)
    ©: Band, 12 Nov 1920, again 5 Mar 1935; ren 13 May 1948,
        again Fischer 12 Apr 1962.
        Orch, 19 Jan 1921; ren 13 May 1948.
        BBB#3.

"High Tower" - march (1933)
    ©: Band, 6 Sep 1933; ren Fischer 15 Sep 1960.
        BBB#4.

"Hiland" - march (1937)
    ©: Band, 16 Aug 1937; ren Fischer 3 Sep 1964.
        BBB#4.

"Idle Fancy" - serenade (1923)
    ©: Band, 15 Jan 1923, again 5 Mar 1935; ren 14 Jly 1950.
        Orch, 10 Jan 1923; ren 28 Feb 1951.
        BBB#1, BOF#1.

"Improvement" - march (1917)
    ©: Band, 13 Jan 1917, again 5 Mar 1935; ren 2 Dec 1944,
        again Fischer 12 Apr 1962.
        BBB#3.

"Indian Boy" - fox trot (1923)
    ©: Band, 15 Jan 1923, again 5 Mar 1935; ren 14 Jly 1950,
        again Fischer 12 Apr 1962.
        Orch, 10 Nov 1923; ren 28 Feb 1951.
        BBB#1, BOF#1.

"Janet" - waltz (1937)
    ©: Band, 16 Aug 1937; ren Fischer 3 Sep 1964.
        BBB#4.

"Knighthood" - march (1937)
    ©: Band, 17 May 1937; ren Fischer 24 Jly 1964.
        BBB#4.

"Laurel" - march (1930)
    ©: Band, 19 Jly 1930, again 5 Mar 1935; ren Fischer 1
        Aug 1957, again Fischer 12 Apr 1962.
        Orch, 3 Oct 1931; not ren.
        BBB#3.

"Little Arab" - fox trot (1926)
    ©: Band, 17 Mar 1926, again 5 Mar 1935; ren Fischer 9
        Sep 1953, again Fischer 12 Apr 1962.
        Orch, 14 Oct 1926; ren Fischer 19 Oct 1953.
        BBB#2, BOF#2.

"The Little Grey Church" - serenade (1923)
    ©: Band, 15 Jan 1923, again 5 Mar 1935; ren 14 Jly 1950,

again Fischer 12 Apr 1962.
Orch, 10 Nov 1923; ren 28 Feb 1951.
BBB#1, BOF#1.

"Little Marie" - waltz (1926)
ⓒ: Band, 17 Mar 1926, again 5 Mar 1935; ren Fischer 9
Sept 1953, again Fischer 12 Apr 1962.
Orch, 14 Oct 1926; ren Fischer 19 Oct 1953.
BBB#2, BOF#2.

"Little Rastus" - characteristic piece (1920)
ⓒ: Band, 2 Mar 1920, again 5 Mar 1935; ren Fischer 12
Apr 1962.
Orch, 3 Oct 1931; not ren.
BBB#3.

"Maybell" - waltz (1931)
ⓒ: Band, 19 Feb 1931, again 5 Mar 1935; ren Fischer 12
Apr 1962.
Orch, 30 Oct 1931; not ren.
BBB#3.

"Military Escort" - march (1923)
ⓒ: Band, 15 Jan 1923, again 5 Mar 1935; ren 14 Jly 1950,
again Fischer 12 Apr 1962.
Orch, 10 Nov 1923; ren Fischer 28 Feb 1951.
BBB#1, BOF#1.

"Mister Joe" - march one-step and two-step (1923)
ⓒ: Band, 15 Jan 1923, again 5 Mar 1935; ren 14 Jly 1950,
again Fischer 12 Apr 1962.
Orch, 10 Nov 1923; ren 28 Feb 1951.
BBB#1, BOF#1.

"Mutual" - march (1923)
ⓒ: Band, 15 Jan 1923, again 5 Mar 1935; ren 14 Jly 1950,
again Fischer 12 Apr 1962.
Orch, 10 Nov 1923; ren 28 Feb 1951.
BBB#1, BOF#1.

"Normal" - march (1923)
ⓒ: Band, 15 Jan 1923, again 5 Mar 1935; ren 14 Jan 1950,
again Fischer 12 Apr 1962.
Orch, 10 Nov 1923; ren 28 Feb 1951.
BBB#1, BOF#1.

"Norma's Dream" - waltz (1923)
ⓒ: Band, 27 Jan 1923, again 5 Mar 1935; ren Fischer 12
Apr 1962.
Orch, 10 Nov 1953; ren 28 Feb 1951.
BBB#1, BOF#1.

"Pivot Man" - march (1937)
ⓒ: Band, 20 May 1937; ren Fischer 24 Jly 1964.
BBB#4.

"Power" - march (1926)

© : Band, 17 Mar 1926, again 5 Mar 1935; ren Fischer 5
    Sep 1953, again Fischer 12 Apr 1962.
    Orch, 14 Oct 1926; ren Fischer 19 Oct 1953.
    BBB#2, BOF#2.

"Precision" - march (1926)
© : Band, 17 Mar 1926, again 5 Mar 1935; ren Fischer 9
    Sep 1953, again Fischer 12 Apr 1962.
    Orch, 14 Oct 1926, ren Fischer 19 Oct 1953.
    BBB#2, BOF#2.

"Proclar" - march (1937)
© : Band, 17 May 1937; ren Fischer 3 Sep 1964.
    BBB#4.

"Progress" - march (1918)
© : Band, 5 Jly 1918, again 5 Mar 1935; ren 30 Nov 1935,
    again Fischer 12 Apr 1962.
    Orch, 3 Oct 1931; not ren.
    BBB#3.

"Project" - march (1923)
© : Band, 15 Jan 1923, again 5 Mar 1935; ren 14 Jly 1950,
    again Fischer 12 Apr 1962.
    Orch, 10 Nov 1923; ren 28 Feb 1951.
    BBB#1, BOF#1.

"Put and Take" - novelty (1937)
© : Band, 16 Aug 1937; ren Fischer 3 Sep 1964.
    BBB#4.

"Sabo" - march (1926)
© : Band, 17 Mar 1926, again 5 Mar 1935; ren Fischer 9
    Sep 1953, again Fischer 12 Apr 1962.
    Orch, 14 Oct 1926; ren Fischer 19 Oct 1953.
    BBB#2, BOF#2.

"Safety" - march (1923)
© : Band, 15 Jan 1923, again 5 Mar 1935; ren 14 Jly 1950,
    again Fischer 12 Apr 1962.
    Orch, 10 Nov 1923; ren 28 Feb 1951.
    BBB#1, BOF#1.

"Service" - march (1921)
© : Band, 10 Oct 1921, again 5 Mar 1935; ren 3 Jan 1949,
    again Fischer 12 Apr 1962.
    Orch, 20 Oct 1931; not ren.
    BBB#3.

"Sola" - fox trot (1926)
© : Band, 17 Mar 1926, again 5 Mar 1935; ren Fischer 9
    Sep 1953, again Fischer 12 Apr 1962.
    Orch, 14 Oct 1926; ren Fischer 19 Oct 1953.
    BBB#2, BOF#2.

"Stop" - fox trot novelty (1923)
© : Band, 15 Jan 1923, again 5 Mar 1935; ren 14 Jly 1950,

again Fischer 12 Apr 1962.
Orch, 10 Nov 1923; ren 28 Feb 1951.
BBB#1, BOF#1.

"Success" - march (1909)
ⓒ: Band, 10 May 1909, again 5 Mar 1935; ren Fischer 12
Apr 1962.
Orch, 5 Feb 1912; ren 1 Nov 1939.
BBB#3.

"Summit" - march (1923)
ⓒ: Band, 15 Jan 1923, again 5 Mar 1935; ren 14 Jly 1950,
again Fischer 12 Apr 1962.
Orch, 10 Nov 1923; ren 28 Feb 1951.
BBB#1, BOF#1.

"System" - march (1937)
ⓒ: Band, 16 Aug 1937; ren Fischer 3 Sep 1964.
BBB#4.

"Vera" - waltz (1937)
ⓒ: Band, 16 Aug 1937; ren Fischer 3 Sep 1964.
BBB#4.

"Village Chimes" - waltz ("Chimes of Love") (1926)
ⓒ: Band, 17 Mar 1926, again 5 Mar 1935; ren Fischer 9
Sep 1953, again Fischer 12 Apr 1962.
Orch, 14 Oct 1926; ren Fischer 19 Oct 1953.
BBB#2, BOF#2.

"Welcome" - march (1912)
ⓒ: Band, 12 Sep 1912, again 5 Mar 1935; ren 19 Jun 1940,
again Fischer 12 Apr 1962.
Orch, 3 Oct 1931; not ren.
BBB#3.

"Yare" - overture (1937)
ⓒ: Band, 16 Aug 1937; ren Fischer 3 Sep 1964.
BBB#4.

"Zenith - overture (1923)
ⓒ: Band, 15 Jan 1923, again 5 Mar 1935; ren 14 Jly 1950,
again Fischer 12 Apr 1962.
Orch, 10 Nov 1923; ren 28 Feb 1951.
BBB#1, BOF#1.

MUSIC COMPOSED BY HENRY FILLMORE
UNDER THE PSEUDONYM RAY HALL

"Cupid's Dart" - waltz (1912)
ⓒ: Orch, 6 Jan 1912; not ren.

"The Merry Makers" - march (1912)
ⓒ: Band, 8 Apr 1912; ren 1 Nov 1939.
Orch, same.

"Our Waving Colors" - march (1914)
  ©: Band, 18 Jun 1914; ren 25 Mar 1942.

MUSIC COMPOSED BY HENRY FILLMORE
UNDER THE PSEUDONYM HARRY HARTLEY

"Gaiety Polka" - solo for cornet, trombone or baritone horn
    (1912)
  ©: Solo instrument and piano, 6 Jan 1912; ren 1 Nov 1939.
      Solo instrument and band, 4 Mar 1912; ren 1 Nov 1939.

"Mabel Polka" - solo for cornet, trombone or baritone horn
    (1912)
  ©: Solo instrument and piano, 22 Jly 1912; ren 19 Jun
      1940.

"Polka Militaire" - solo for cornet, trombone or baritone
    horn (1912)
  ©: Solo instrument and piano, 22 Jly 1912; ren 19 Jun
      1940.

"Triumph Polka" - solo for cornet, trombone or baritone horn
    (1912)
  ©: Solo instrument and piano, 4 Mar 1912; ren 1 Nov
      1939.

"Valse Fantastic" - solo for cornet, trombone or baritone
    horn (1912)
  ©: Solo instrument and piano, 5 Feb 1912; ren Henry
      Fillmore 1 Nov 1939.

"Whirlpool Polka" - solo for cornet, trombone or baritone
    horn (1912)
  ©: Solo instrument and piano, 8 Apr 1912; ren 1 Nov
      1939.

MUSIC COMPOSED BY HENRY FILLMORE
UNDER THE PSEUDONYM AL HAYES

"Altos to the Front" - trio for alto horns (1912)
    Not ©. Band.

"America Exultant - march (1917)
    Incorporating the traditional air "America"
  ©: Band, 21 May 1917; ren 2 Dec 1944.

"The American" - march and two-step (1911)
  ©: Band, 14 Nov 1911; ren Henry Fillmore 28 Jan 1939.
      Orch, same.

"Banner of Democracy" - march (1917)
    Incorporating the national air, "Columbia the Gem of the
      Ocean" ("Red, White and Blue")

ⓒ: Band, 21 May 1917; ren 2 Dec 1944.

"The Black Mask" - march (1914)
    ⓒ: Band, 1 May 1914; ren 25 Mar 1942.
        Orch, 17 Jan 1916; ren 8 Nov 1943.

"Clovernook" - schottische (1914)
    ⓒ: Band, 1 May 1914; ren 25 Mar 1942.
        Orch, 4 Nov 1916; ren 5 Jun 1944.

"The Courier" - march and two-step (1914)
    ⓒ: Band, 1 May 1914; ren 25 Mar 1942.
        Orch, 17 Jan 1916; ren 8 Nov 1943.

"Cradle of Liberty" - march (1905)
    ⓒ: Band, 15 Jun 1905; ren 17 May 1933.

"Determination" - overture (1917)
    ⓒ: Band, 13 Jan 1917; ren 2 Dec 1944.
        Orch, 12 Mar 1917; ren 2 Dec 1944.

"Dew Drops" - mazurka or three-step (1908)
    ⓒ: Band, 28 Aug 1908; ren 3 Aug 1936.
        Orch, 28 Aug 1908; not ren.

"Duke Street" - march (1911)
    Based on the hymns, "The Half Has Never Been Told" and
        "Duke Street"
    ⓒ: Band, 5 Jun 1911; ren 28 Jan 1939.

"Emerald Waltzes" (1908)
    ⓒ: Band, 17 Apr 1908; not ren.
        Orch, same.

"Empyrean" - overture (1919)
    ⓒ: Band, 28 Apr 1919; ren 6 Oct 1946.

"Evening Breezes" - serenade (1914)
    ⓒ: Band, 1 May 1914; ren 25 Mar 1942.
        Orch, 4 Nov 1916; ren 5 May 1944.

"Extempore" - overture (1912)
    ⓒ: Band, 12 May 1912; not ren.

"Exuberance" - overture (1915)
    ⓒ: Band, 8 May 1915; ren 23 Oct 1942.
        Orch, same.

"Fall Roses" - waltz (1906)
    ⓒ: Band, 11 Jan 1906; not ren.
        Orch, same.
        Piano, 23 Jan 1906; not ren.

"Flag of Humanity" - march (1917)
    Incorporating "The Star Spangled Banner"
    ⓒ: Band, 1 May 1917; ren 2 Dec 1944.
        Orch, same.

"Los Flores" - tango Argentine (1914)
    ⓒ: Band, 1 May 1914; ren 25 Mar 1942.

Orch, 14 Feb 1916; ren 8 Nov 1943.

"Fraternity" - march (1910)
ⓒ: Band, 5 Jly 1910; ren 3 Feb 1938.
Orch, 1 Oct 1910, ren 3 Feb 1938.

"Gibraltar" - overture (1914)
ⓒ: Band, 1 May 1914; ren 25 Mar 1942.
Orch, 14 Feb 1916; ren 8 Nov 1943.

"The Glencoe" - march and two-step (1914)
ⓒ: Band, 1 May 1914; ren 25 Mar 1942.

"Go To It" - one-step, two-step or turkey trot (1914)
ⓒ: Band, 1 May 1914; ren 25 Mar 1942.
Orch, 4 Nov 1916; ren 5 May 1944.

"Good Citizenship" - march and two-step (1907)
ⓒ: Band, 20 Apr 1907; not ren.
Orch, same.

"The Gypsy Festival" - overture (1924)
ⓒ: Band, 26 Feb 1924; ren Henry Fillmore 30 Jan 1952.
Orch, same.

"The Herald" - march and two-step (1914)
ⓒ: Band, 1 May 1914; ren 25 Mar 1942.
Orch, 4 Nov 1916; ren 5 May 1944.

"Inspiration" - overture (1907)
ⓒ: Band, 20 Apr 1907; ren 22 Mar 1935.
Orch, 30 Dec 1907; ren 28 Dec 1935.

"Joyful Greeting" - march (1918)
By John Littleton and Al Hayes
Incorporating the song "Home Sweet Home"
ⓒ: Band, 11 Dec 1918; ren 19 Jly 1946.
Orch, same.

"Juliet" - waltz (1914)
ⓒ: Band, 1 May 1914; ren 25 Mar 1942.
Orch, 8 Dec 1915; ren 5 Apr 1943.

"A Little Bit of Pop" - humoresque (1918)
Variations on the song "Pop Goes the Weasel"
Not ⓒ. Band.

"Longtone" - march (1920)
ⓒ: Band, 2 Mar 1920; ren 21 Jly 1947.

"March of the Mighty" (1912)
ⓒ: Band, 22 Jly 1912; ren 19 Jun 1940.
Orch, same.

"Mariana" - caprice (1907)
ⓒ: Band, 30 Dec 1907; not ren.
Orch, same.

"The Merrimac" - march and two-step (1914)
ⓒ: Band, 1 May 1914; ren 25 Mar 1942.

Orch, 4 Nov 1916; ren 5 May 1944.

"The Monitor" - march (1914)
ⓒ: Band, 1 May 1914; ren 25 Mar 1942.
Orch, 4 Nov 1916; ren 5 May 1944.

"Necoid" - march (1921)
ⓒ: Band, 10 Oct 1921; ren 3 Jan 1949.

"The North Pole" - overture (1910)
ⓒ: Band, 4 Feb 1910; ren 3 Feb 1938.

"Old Kentucky Home" - march (1907)
Incorporating the song "My Old Kentucky Home"
ⓒ: Band, 17 Aug 1907; ren 14 Jun 1935.

"The Old Oaken Bucket" - march (1906)
Incorporating the song "The Old Oaken Bucket"
Not ⓒ. Band.

"The Only Tune the Band Could Play Was Auld Lang Syne" -
Humoresque (1911)
ⓒ: Band, 20 Nov 1911; ren 28 Jan 1939.
Orch, same.

"Onward Christian Soldiers" - march (1913)
Incorporating the hymn "Onward Christian Soldiers"
ⓒ: Band, 29 May 1913; ren 27 Mar 1941.
Orch, same.

"Organ Echoes" - serenade (1914)
ⓒ: Band, 1 May 1914; ren 25 Mar 1942.
Orch, 9 Dec 1915; ren 5 Apr 1943.

"Peace and Prosperity" - march (1906)
ⓒ: Band, 22 Aug 1906; ren 3 Aug 1934.
Orch, 31 Dec 1906; not ren.

"The Pirate" - march (1908)
ⓒ: Band, 21 Dec 1908; not ren.

"Pond Lilies" - waltz (1914)
ⓒ: Band, 1 May 1914; ren 25 Mar 1942.
Orch, 4 Nov 1916; ren 5 May 1944.

"Queen of May" - schottische (1906)
ⓒ: Band, 11 Jan 1906; not ren.
Orch, same.
Piano, 25 Jan 1906; not ren.

"Rocked in the Cradle of the Deep" - march (1908)
Incorporating the song, "Rocked in the Cradle of the Deep"
ⓒ: Band, 28 Feb 1908; ren 17 Feb 1936.

"Sinfonia" - march and two-step (1914)
ⓒ: Band, 1 May 1914; ren 25 Mar 1942.
Orch, 4 Nov 1916; ren 5 May 1944.

"Softly Peals the Organ" - serenade (1921)
ⓒ: Band, 5 Jan 1921; not ren.

"Solo Pomposo" - tuba solo (1911)
   ⓒ: Tuba and band, 12 Dec 1911; ren 28 Jan 1939.
      Tuba and piano, same.

"Southern Pastime" - march and two-step (1908)
   ⓒ: Band, 28 Feb 1908; ren 17 Feb 1936.
      Orch, 28 Feb 1908; not ren.

"Spirit of the Age" - overture (1920)
   ⓒ: Band, 8 Mar 1920; not ren.
      Orch, same.

"Under Arms" - march (1904)
   ⓒ: Band, 18 Apr 1904; ren 30 Jan 1932.
      Piano, 6 Jun 1907; not ren.

"United Service" - march (1917)
   Incorporating the songs "Dixie" and "Marching Through
     Georgia"
   ⓒ: Band, 1 May 1917; ren 2 Dec 1944.

"The Universe" - march (1921)
   Not ⓒ. Band.

"Visions" - trio (1911)
   For three alto horns or two alto horns and baritone horn
   ⓒ: Solo instruments and band, 5 May 1911; ren 28 Jan
      1939.

"Vivian" - hesitation waltz (1914)
   ⓒ: Band, 1 May 1914; ren 25 Mar 1942.
      Orch, 4 Nov 1916; ren 5 May 1944.

MUSIC COMPOSED BY HENRY FILLMORE
UNDER THE PSEUDONYM WILL HUFF

"Alamo" - march (1916)
   ⓒ: Band, 26 Jun 1916; ren 8 Nov 1943.
      Orch, 3 Dec 1918; ren 19 Jly 1946.
      HPEBB, HPEOF.

"La Albuera" - spanish waltz (1916)
   ⓒ: Band, 26 Jun 1916; ren 8 Nov 1943.
      Orch, 3 Dec 1918; ren 19 Jly 1946.
      HPEBB, HPEOF.

"La Cascade" - overture (1916)
   ⓒ: Band, 26 Jun 1916; ren 8 Nov 1943.
      Orch, 3 Dec 1918; ren 19 Jly 1946.
      HPEBB, HPEOF.

"Dynamic" - overture (1916)
   ⓒ: Band, 26 Jun 1916; ren 8 Nov 1943.
      Orch, 3 Dec 1918; ren 19 Jly 1946.
      HPEBB, HPEOF.

"Go" - galop (1916)
  ©: Band, 26 Jun 1916; ren 8 Nov 1943.
      Orch, 3 Dec 1918; ren 19 Jly 1946.
      HPEBB, HPEOF.

"Golden Plume" - march (1916)
  ©: Band, 26 Jun 1916; ren 8 Nov 1943.
      Orch, 3 Dec 1918; ren 19 Jly 1946.
      HPEBB, HPEOF.

"Higham March" (1903)
  ©: Band, 4 Sep 1903; not ren.
      Orch, 18 Apr 1904; not ren.

"March of the Blue Brigade" (1904)
  "Dedicated to the United States Army"
  ©: Band, 18 Apr 1904; not ren.

MUSIC COMPOSED BY HENRY FILLMORE
UNDER THE PSEUDONYM HENRIETTA MOORE

"Twilight Song" (1917)
  Words by Eleanor Allen Schroll
  ©: Vocal and piano, 14 May 1917; ren 2 Dec 1944.
      Also publ as solo for cornet, trombone or baritone
      horn with band but not ©.

ARRANGEMENTS MADE UNDER THE NAME HENRY FILLMORE

"Ah, Sweet Mystery of Life" from *Naughty Marietta* (1932)
  (Victor Herbert)
  Not © or publ. Vocal and band.

"Alma Mater" (1948)
  (Lampe and Asdurian)
  ©: Vocal and band, U of M 23 Aug 1948; not ren.

"America" - national air (1934)
  (Traditional)
  ©: Band, 5 Sep 1934; ren Fischer 21 Sep 1961.

"Babes in Toyland" - selections from the operetta (1928)
  (Victor Herbert)
  Not © or publ. Band.

"The Beautiful Garden of Prayer" - hymn (1924)
  (J.H. Fillmore)
  Solo for cornet, trombone, baritone horn or saxophone
  ©: Band, 14 May 1924; ren 24 Mar 1952.
      Orch, 9 Jun 1924; ren 24 Mar 1952.

"The Bells of St. Mary's" - serenade (1932)
  (M. Emmett Adams)

Not ©️ or publ. Band.

"Beyond the Blue Horizon" - song (1933)
  (Richard A. Whiting, W. Franke Harling and Leo Robin)
  Not ©️ or publ. Vocal and band.

"Billy Sunday's Successful Songs" - overture (1916)
  Medley of 7 hymns
  ©️: Band, 6 Jan 1916; ren 8 Nov 1943.
    Orch, same.

"Champ Clark's Congress" - march (1911)
  (Will Huff)
  Band.
  For ©️ information see Part Two.

"Chicken Reel" (no date)
  (Joseph M. Daly)
  Not ©️ or publ. Band.

Concertina for Clarinet (1933)
  (Carl Maria von Weber)
  Not ©️ or publ. Clarinet and band.

"Down South" - concert piece (1928)
  (W.H. Myddleton)
  Not ©️ or publ. Band.

"Dull Razor" - blues (1933)
  (G.H. Huffine)
  Not ©️ or publ. Band.

"Eleanor" - waltzes (1912)
  (Will Huff)
  Band; also orch.
  For ©️ information see Part Two.

"Evening Star" from *Tannhauser* (no date)
  (Richard Wagner)
  Not ©️ or publ. Vocal and band.

"Farewell to Arms" - song (1933)
  (Wrubel and Silver)
  Not ©️ or publ. Vocal and band.

"Flight of the Bumblebee" - concert piece (1928)
  (Nicolai Rimsky-Korsakov)
  Not ©️ or publ. Band.

"Gary Owen March" (1904)
  (James M. Fulton)
  ©️: Orch 18 Apr 1904; not ren.

"Giannina Mia" from *The Firefly* (1933)
  (Rudolf Friml)
  Not ©️ or publ. Vocal and band.

The Gloria Band Book (1915)
  Collection of 67 hymns and gospel songs arranged for
    band, adaptable for brass quartet
  ©️: Band, 16 Aug 1915; ren 5 Apr 1943.

"Hail to the Spirit of Miami U" - pep song (1948)
(Clark and Kennedy)
ⓒ: Vocal and band, U of M 23 Aug 1948; not ren.

Hymns for Today (1920)
Collection of 332 hymns and gospel songs arranged for
small orchestra
ⓒ: Orch, 1 May 1920; ren 21 Jly 1947.

"Inflammatus" from *Stabat Mater* (1933)
(Gioacchino Rossini)
Not ⓒ or publ. Vocal and band.

"I'll Wear a White Flower For You, Mother Dear" - song (1914
& 1916)
(Charles M. Fillmore)
ⓒ: Vocal and orch, 3 Apr 1914; ren 27 Mar 1942.
Vocal and band, 4 Nov 1916; ren 5 May 1944.

"Iowa Corn Song" (1950)
(Edward Riley)
Not ⓒ or publ. Band.

"The Jollier" - march and two-step (1906)
(Warner Crosby)
ⓒ: Band, 12 Mar 1906; not ren.
Orch, same.
Piano, same.

"Just a Cottage Small by a Waterfall" - song (1933)
(James F. Hanley and G. DeSylva)
Not ⓒ or publ. Vocal and band.

"Keep It Rollin'" - pep song (1948)
(Eddie Baumgarten)
Not ⓒ or publ. Band.

"A Kiss in the Dark" from *Orange Blossoms* (1930)
(Victor Herbert)
Not ⓒ or publ. Vocal and band.

"Kiss Me Again" from *Mlle Modiste* (1933)
(Victor Herbert)
Not ⓒ or publ. Vocal and band.

"Language of the Soul" - waltzes (no date)
(W.H. Scouton)
Not ⓒ or publ. Band.

"Life and Liberty" - march (1908)
(Will Huff)
Band.
For ⓒ information see Part Two.

"Light Cavalry" - overture (1922)
(Franz von Suppe)
ⓒ: Band, 13 Feb 1922; ren 30 Jun 1949.

"March Endeavor" (1909)
(Will Huff)

Band.
For ©️ information see Part Two.

"March of the 31st" (no date)
(A.F. Weldon)
Not ©️ or publ. Band.

"Maytime" - selections from the operetta (1936)
(Sigmund Romberg)
Not ©️ or publ. Band.

"Miami Fight" - pep song (no date)
(Rex Hall)
Not ©️ or publ. Band.

"Minute Waltz" (1928)
(Frederick Chopin)
Not ©️ or publ. Band.

"Miserere" from *Il Trovatore* (no date)
(Giuseppe Verdi)
Not ©️ or publ. Vocal and band.

"Morning, Noon and Night" [in Vienna] - overture (1922)
(Franz von Suppe)
©️: Band, 9 Jun 1922; ren 30 Jun 1949.

"My Darling" [and others] - medley (1933)
(Richard Myers [and others])
Not ©️ or publ. Band.

"National Emblem" - march (no date)
(E.E. Bagley)
Not ©️ or publ. Band.

"The Night Riders" - patrol (1908)
(Will Huff)
Band; also orch.
For ©️ information see Part Two.

"Oh, That Kiss" - song (no date)
(By ?)
Not ©️ or publ. Vocal and band.

"The Old Gray Mare" - variations (no date)
(Warner and Panella)
Not ©️ or publ. Band.

"Old Man River and Others" - concert piece (no date)
(Jerome Kern and others)
Medley of popular songs
Not ©️ or publ. Band.

"On the Mall" - march (no date)
(Edwin Franko Goldman)
Not ©️ or publ. Band.

"One Alone" from *The Desert Song* (1933)
(Sigmund Romberg)

Not © or publ. Vocal and band.

"Peanuts" - song (no date)
   (Marion Sunshine)
   Not © or publ. Band.

"Poet and Peasant" - overture (1922)
   (Franz von Suppe)
   © : Band, 1 Mar 1922; ren 30 Jun 1949.

"Polka Majestic" (1906)
   (Walter Brister)
   © : Band, 31 Dec 1906; not ren.
       Orch, same.

"Popular Song Choruses" - concert piece (1933)
   Medley of popular songs
   Not © or publ. Band.

"Puritani" - clarinet solo (1935)
   (L. Bassi)
   Not © or publ. Clarinet solo with band.

Quartets and Choruses for Men (1913)
   26 arrangements by Henry Fillmore in a collection of 221
       hymns, gospel songs, songs and national airs
   © : Mens' voices, 15 Dec 1913; ren Henry Fillmore 27
           Mar 1941.

"Ragamuffin Rag" - march and two-step (1913)
   (Will Huff)
   Band; orch.
   For © information see Part Two.

"Reveille" - bugle call, harmonized (1934)
   (Traditional)
   © : Band, 5 Sep 1934; ren Fischer 21 Sep 1961.

Rhapsody in Blue (1934)
   (George Gershwin)
   Not © or publ. Band.

"Rigoletto" - selections from the opera (1933)
   (Giuseppe Verdi)
   Not © or publ. Band.

"A Rural Celebration" - descriptive piece (1909)
   (Will Huff)
   Band.
   For © information see Part Two.

"Sacred Orchestra Selections No. 1" (1908)
   Medley of 5 hymns
   © : Orch, 28 Aug 1908; ren 3 Aug 1936.

"Sacred Orchestra Selections No. 2" (1912)
   Medley of 7 hymns
   © : Orch, 6 Jan 1912; ren 1 Nov 1939.

"Salute to Uncle Sam" - march (1908)
   (Will Huff)
   Band.
   For ©️ information see Part Two.

"Schön Rosmarin" - caprice (1930)
   (Fritz Kreisler)
   Not ©️ or publ. Band.

"The Show Boy" - march (1911)
   (Will Huff)
   Band; also orch.
   For ©️ information see Part Two.

"The Show Girl" - march (1916)
   (Will Huff)
   Band.
   For ©️ information see Part Two.

"Silver Bell Waltz" (1907)
   (T.L. Eells)
   ©️ : Band, Wurlitzer 19 Apr 1907; not ren.

"The Song I Love" (1930)
   (DeSylva, Brown, Henderson and Conrad)
   Not ©️ or publ. Band.

Songs of Praise (1912)
   Collection of 129 hymns and gospel songs arranged for
      small orchestra
   ©️ : Orch, 10 Dec 1912; ren 1 Nov 1939.

"Square Deal" - march (1908)
   (Will Huff)
   Band.
   For ©️ information see Part Two.

"The Squealer" - marchio circusosio (1912)
   (Will Huff)
   Band.
   For ©️ information see Part Two.

"The Star Spangled Banner" - American national anthem (1934)
   (Francis Scott Key)
   ©️ : Band, 5 Sep 1934; ren Fischer 21 Sep 1961.

"Stormy Weather" [and others] - concert piece (1933)
   (Harold Arlen [and others])
   Medley of popular songs
   Not ©️ or publ. Band.

"Strike for Freedom" - march and two-step (1906)
   (C.G. Culver)
   ©️ : Band, 22 Aug 1906; not ren.
        Orch, 31 Dec 1906; not ren.

"Sunny Side Up" - selections from the movie (1930)
   (Ray Henderson)

Not © or publ. Band.

"Sweethearts" - selection from the operetta (1928)
   (Victor Herbert)
   Not © or publ. Band.

"Taps" - bugle call, harmonized (1934)
   (Traditional)
   ©: Band, 5 Sep 1934; ren Fischer 21 Sep 1961.

"Them Basses" - march (ca. 1932)
   (G.H. Huffine)
   Not © or publ. Band.

"Trees" - song (1933)
   (Oscar Rassbach and Joyce Kilmer)
   Not © or publ. Vocal and band.

"Try a Little Tenderness" [and others] - concert piece (1933)
   (Woods, Campbell and Connelly [and others])
   Medley of popular songs
   Not © or publ. Band.

"Two Hearts in Waltz Time" - song (1933)
   (Robert Stolz)
   Not © or publ. Vocal and band.

"Under the Double Eagle" - march (1929)
   (Josef Franz Wagner)
   Not © or publ. Band.

"Villanelle" - song (1933)
   (Eva Dell' Acqua)
   Not © or publ. Vocal and band.

"Under Northern Skies" - march and two-step (1906)
   (Albert Moquin)
   ©: Band, 31 Dec 1906; not ren.
      Orch, same.

"Victor Herbert's Favorites" - medley (1928)
   (Victor Herbert)
   Not © or publ. Band.

"We're in the Money" [and others] - medley (1933)
   (Harry Warren [and others])
   Not © or publ. Band.

"Will You Remember?" from *Maytime* (1933)
   (Sigmund Romberg)
   Not © or publ. Vocal and band.

"Young and Healthy" - song (1933)
   (Harry Warren)
   Not © or publ. Band.

"4 Minutes in Grand Opera" - fox trot (1932)
   Medley of various opera selections
   Not © or publ. Band.

"42nd Street" - selections from the musical (1933)
   (Harry Warner)
   Not ©️ or publ. Band.

Will Huff Band Book (1913)
   Collection of 16 compositions by Will Huff, arranged for
      band.
   For listing and ©️ information see Part Two.

Huff Par-Excel Band Book (1916)
   10 of the 16 Will Huff compositions, arranged for band,
      as follows:
      "Cotton Top Rag" - march and two-step
      "The Floral Parade" - march
      "Fort Chester" - march and two-step
      "Georgiana" - waltzes
      "Melody to Youth" - serenade
      "The Peerless" - march
      "The Poet's Dream" - serenade
      "The Premium" - march
      "Rosida" - waltz
      "Tuxedo" - march
   For ©️ information see Part Two.

Plus numerous compositions and arrangements of youthful
   years. Not ©️ or publ.

Plus several arrangements for band made for Mr. John A.
   Broekhoven while a student at the College of Music of
   Cincinnati, 1901-02. Not ©️ or publ.

Plus numerous piano and/or choral arrangements made for
   Fillmore Brothers Company publications between 1901 and
   1920.

Plus numerous arrangements made for theater orchestras in
   Cincinnati between 1905 and 1911. Not ©️ or publ.

Plus numerous arrangements for small orchestra made for cer-
   emonials of the High Noon Lodge, Free and Accepted Ma-
   sons, Cincinnati, between 1916 and 1930. Not ©️ or
   publ.

ARRANGEMENTS MADE BY HENRY FILLMORE
UNDER THE PSEUDONYM HARRY HARTLEY

"Four Brass Quartets" - songs (1911)
   "Robin Adair" (traditional), "The Old Oaken Bucket" (Sam-
   uel Woodworth), "How Can I Leave Thee" (traditional) and
   "Dixie Land" (Daniel Decatur Emmett)
   For four cornets or two cornets, alto horn and baritone
      horn
   ©️ : Brass quartet, 14 Nov 1911; not ren.

"Somewhere Sometime" - hymn (1912)
   (Charles H. Gabriel)
   Solo for cornet, trombone or baritone horn
   ©: Solo instrument and piano, 6 Jan 1912; not ren.

"Tell Mother I'll Be There" - song (1912)
   (Charles M. Fillmore)
   Solo for cornet, trombone or baritone horn
   ©: Solo instrument and piano, 6 Jan 1912; not ren.

ARRANGEMENTS MADE BY HENRY FILLMORE
UNDER THE PSEUDONYM AL HAYES

"Aida" - selections from the opera (1917)
   (Giuseppe Verdi)
   ©: Band, 12 Mar 1917; ren 2 Dec 1944.

"America" - national air (1917 & 1919)
   (Traditional)
   ©: Orch, 22 Dec 1917; ren 15 Apr 1945.
       Band, 2 Jun 1919; ren 6 Oct 1946.

"Ben Bolt" - song (1914 & 1917)
   (Nelson Kneass)
   Duet for two cornets or cornet and trombone
   ©: Solo instruments and orch, 8 Oct 1914; ren 2 Jly
       1942.
       Solo instruments and band, 12 Mar 1917; ren 2 Dec
       1944.

"The Best-Loved Irish Melodies" - concert piece (1918)
   Medley of 9 Irish songs
   ©: Band, 2 Feb 1918; ren 30 Nov 1945.
       Orch, same.

"The Best-Loved Southern Melodies" - concert piece (1915)
   Medley of 6 plantation songs
   ©: Band, 7 Apr 1915; ren 23 Oct 1942.
       Orch, same.

"The Blue-Bells of Scotland" - Scottish national air (1918)
   (Traditional)
   ©: Band, 20 Nov 1918; not ren.
       Orch, same.

"Bohemian Girl" - selections from the opera (1910 & 1915)
   (Michael William Balfe)
   ©: Band, 4 Apr 1910; ren 3 Feb 1938.
       Orch, 9 Mar 1915; not ren.

"The Booster" - march (1913)
   (J.G. Klein)
   ©: Band, 1 Feb 1913; ren 16 Sep 1940.
       Orch, same.

"La Brabanconne" - Belgian national air (1918)
  (F. Campenhout)
   ⓒ: Band, 20 Nov 1918; ren 19 Jly 1946.
     Orch, same.

"The British Grenadiers" - British national air (1918)
  (Traditional)
   ⓒ: Band, 20 Nov 1918; not ren.
     Orch, 20 Nov 1918; ren 19 Jly 1946)

"Carmen" - selections from the opera (1913)
  (Georges Bizet)
   ⓒ: Band, 22 Apr 1913; ren 16 Sep 1940.

"Darling Nellie Gray" - song (1919)
  (Benjamin R. Hanby)
   ⓒ: Band, 2 Jun 1919; ren 6 Oct 1946.

"Dixie" - song (1919)
  (Daniel Decatur Emmett)
   ⓒ: Band, 30 Aug 1919; ren 6 Oct 1946.

"Faust" - selections from the opera (1910)
  (Charles Gounod)
   ⓒ: Band, 4 May 1910; ren 3 Feb 1938.

"Firm and Steady" - march and two-step (1906)
  (Albert L. Moquin)
   ⓒ: Band, 31 Dec 1906; not ren.
     Orch, same.

"Friendship" - march and two-step (1913)
  (William M. Talbott)
   ⓒ: Orch, 10 Dec 1913; ren 27 Mar 1941.

"Garibaldi Hymn" - Italian national air (1918)
  (Traditional)
   ⓒ: Band, 20 Nov 1918; not ren.
     Orch, same.

"Hail Columbia" - American national air (1918)
  (Philip Phile)
   ⓒ: Band, 28 Nov 1918; ren 19 Jly 1946.

"I Love to Tell the Story" - overture (1911)
  Medley of 6 hymns
   ⓒ: Orch, 3 Jan 1911; not ren.

"Joy to the World" - overture (1906 & 1910)
  Medley of 6 hymns
   ⓒ: Orch, 30 Apr 1906; ren 20 Apr 1934.
     Band, 3 Jan 1910; not ren.

"Kimygayo" - Japanese national air (1918)
  (Traditional)
   ⓒ: Band, 20 Nov 1918; not ren.
     Orch, 20 Nov 1918; ren 19 Jly 1946.

"Kingdom Coming" - song (1919)
 (Henry Clay Work)
 ⓒ: Band, 30 Aug 1919; ren 6 Oct 1946.

"The Maple Leaf Forever" - Canadian national anthem (1917)
 (Alexander Muir)
 ⓒ: Band, 22 Dec 1917; ren 15 Apr 1945.

"The Marseillaise" - French national anthem (1917)
 (Claude DeLisle)
 ⓒ: Band, 22 Dec 1917; ren 15 Apr 1945.

"Martha" - selections from the opera (1910)
 (Friedrich von Flotow)
 ⓒ: Band, 7 Oct 1910; ren 3 Feb 1938.

"Maryland" ("Maryland, My Maryland") - song (1919)
 (Traditional)
 ⓒ: Band, 30 Aug 1919; ren 6 Oct 1946.

"Old Black Joe and Massas in de Cold Cold Ground" - medley
 march (1906)
 Medley of the two songs
 (Stephen Foster)
 Not ⓒ. Band.

"Piaski's Polish Dance" (1917)
 (Ignace Piaski)
 ⓒ: Band, 21 Jly 1917; ren 15 Apr 1945.

"Quartet from Rigoletto" (1919)
 For 2 cornets and 2 trombones
 (Giuseppe Verdi)
 ⓒ: Solo instruments and band, 2 Jun 1919; not ren.

"Red, White and Blue" ("Columbia the Gem of the Ocean") -
 American national air (1918)
 (David T. Shaw)
 ⓒ: Band, 28 Nov 1918; ren 19 Jly 1946.

"Rule Brittania" - British national air (1918)
 (Traditional)
 ⓒ: Band, 20 Nov 1918; not ren.
  Orch, 20 Nov 1918; ren 19 Jly 1946.

"Salute to the Stars and Stripes" - march (1942)
 (Will Huff)
 Band.
 For ⓒ information see Part Two.

"Scenes from Operaland" - concert piece (1919)
 Excerpts from 5 popular operas
 ⓒ: Band, 30 Aug 1919; ren 6 Oct 1946.

"The Show Girl" - march (1916)
 (Will Huff)
 Orch.
 For ⓒ information see Part Two.

"The Star Spangled Banner" - American national anthem (1917
   & 1919)
   (Francis Scott Key)
   ©: Orch, 22 Dec 1917; ren 15 Apr 1945.
       Band, 2 Jun 1919; ren 6 Oct 1946.

"Tannhauser" - selections from the opera (1913)
   (Richard Wagner)
   ©: Band, 6 Jan 1913; ren 16 Sep 1940.

"There Is a Land Where Summer Skies" - Australian national
   air (1918)
   (Carl Linger)
   ©: Band, 20 Nov 1918; ren 19 Jly 1946.
       Orch, same.

"Three Merry (K)Nights" - overture (1909)
   (A.B. Strauss)
   "To A.B. Strauss' opera"
   ©: Band, 1 Dec 1909; not ren.

"Three Rings" - march (1915)
   (William M. Talbott)
   ©: Band, 11 Feb 1915; ren 23 Oct 1942.
       Orch, same.

"Throw Out the Life-Line" - overture (1912)
   Medley of 6 hymns
   ©: Band, 4 Mar 1912; ren 1 Nov 1939.
       Orch, same.

"Il Trovatore" - selections from the opera (1910)
   (Giuseppe Verdi)
   ©: Band, 10 Jun 1910; ren 3 Feb 1938.

"United We Stand" - concert piece (1915)
   Medley of 10 patriotic pieces
   ©: Band, 10 Jun 1915; not ren.

"When Johnny Comes Marching Home" - song (1917 & 1919)
   (Patrick S. Gilmore, alias Louis Lambert)
   ©: Orch, 22 Dec 1917; ren 15 Apr 1945.
       Band, 2 Jun 1919; ren 6 Oct 1946.

"When Love Shines In" - concert piece (1915)
   Arranged by William J. Kirkpatrick and Al Hayes
   Medley of 6 hymns
   ©: Band, 12 Nov 1915; ren 5 Apr 1943.
       Orch, same.

"When You and I Were Young, Maggie" - song (1914 & 1917)
   (James Austin Butterfield)
   Vocal solo or solo for cornet, trombone or baritone horn
   ©: Vocal and orchestra, 8 Oct 1914; ren 2 Jly 1942.
       Solo instrument and band, 12 Mar 1917; ren 2 Dec
           1944.

Will Huff Orchestra Folio (1914)
    Collection of 16 compositions by Will Huff, arranged for
        orchestra
    For listing and ⓒ information see Part Two.

Huff Par-Excel Orchestra Folio (1918)
    10 of the 16 Will Huff compositions, arranged for or-
        chestra, as follows:
            "Cotton Top Rag" - march and two-step
            "The Floral Parade" - march
            "Fort Chester" - march and two-step
            "Georgiana" - waltzes
            "Melody to Youth" - serenade
            "The Peerless" - march
            "The Poet's Dream" - serenade
            "The Premium" - march
            "Rosida" - waltz
            "Tuxedo" - march
    For ⓒ information see Part Two.

PART TWO

THE MUSIC OF
WILL HUFF

PREFACE TO PART TWO

The sixty-six original compositions of Will Huff listed in Part Two represent all those which the author saw proof of in his research. The total number might exceed ninety, however, because of numerous unpublished pieces believed to have been written by Huff.

The dates appearing in parentheses beside the titles refer to the dates of the first copyrights except in cases where copyrights were not issued. In these cases, the dates of composition or dates of publication are given, if known.

The copyright dates refer to the original editions for band or orchestra which were, in nearly all instances, the only published editions. A few were later published for other instrumentations, but these have not been listed. An example of one of these unlisted editions would be the publication of the "Magneta" overture which was distributed many years later (1941) by the Fillmore Brothers Company in an arrangement for four accordians by Aretta and Howell.

An oddity appearing in a study of copyright registrations was that one of the publishers, Will H. Smith & Son, did not actually copyright three of their four Huff compositions, even though the printed music of all four bore copyright notices.

The Star Music Company, curiously, did not copyright Huff's music. It was learned in a search of the copyright entry card file at the Library of Congress that Huff was just one of Star's contributors lacking copyright protection.

It should be noted that the Fillmore Brothers Company published most of the Huff pieces in both band and orchestra editions but was not consistent in their copyright procedure. The sixteen pieces in the *Huff Par-Excel Band Book* were copyrighted together as a collection on 1 April 1913. But when this collection was later published for orchestra as the *Will Huff Orchestra Folio*, all sixteen pieces were copyrighted individually on 21 January 1914. The copyright renewals were handled similarly.

The Fillmore Brothers Company avoided such confusion when it published a second collection of pieces in 1916. The *Huff Par-Excel Band Book* and its companion publication, the *Huff Par-Excel Orchestra Folio*, were copyrighted as collections only, on 26 June 1916 and 3 December 1918, respectively, and renewed in the same manner.

LEGEND FOR PART TWO

Band	For band
©	Copyright, or copyrigh·ed
FBros	Fillmore Brothers Company (Fillmore Music House), Cincinnati, Ohio
HPEBB	Included in the *Huff Par-Excel Band Book*
HPEOF	Included in the *Huff Par-Excel Orchestra Folio*
Orch	For orchestra
Publ	Publisher, or published
Ren	Renewal of copyright, or renewed
Smith	Will H. Smith & Son, Dixon, Illinois
Star	Star Music Company, Eldred, Pennsylvania
WHBB	Included in the *Will Huff Band Book*
WHOF	Included in the *Will Huff Orchestra Folio*
Wurlitzer	Rudolph Wurlitzer Company, Cincinnati, Ohio

MUSIC COMPOSED BY WILL HUFF

"Battleship Maine March" (1899)
    ©: Band, Wurlitzer 24 Jly 1899; not ren.

"Canadian Club March" (1899)
    ©: Band, Wurlitzer 24 Jly 1899; not ren.

"Champ Clark's Congress" - march (1911)
    ©: Band, FBros 8 Jly 1911; ren FBros 28 Jan 1939.

"Chillicothe High School Band March" (1929)
    Not © or publ. Band.

"Cotton Top Rag" - march and two-step (1916)
    ©: Band, FBros 26 Jun 1916; ren FBros 8 Nov 1943.
        Orch, FBros 3 Dec 1918; ren FBros 19 Jly 1946.
        HPEBB, HPEOF

"Eleanor" - waltzes (1912)
    ©: Band, FBros 22 Jun 1912; ren FBros 19 Jun 1940.
        Orch, same.

"The Emblem March" (probably 1911)
    Not © . Publ Star. Band; orch; also cornet solo with
          piano.

"Eyes of Brown" - schottische (1913)
    ©: Band, FBros 1 Apr 1913; ren FBros 11 Oct 1940.
        Orch, FBros 21 Jan 1914; ren FBros 7 Jan 1942.
        WHBB, WHOF.

"E-Z March" (1921)
    Not © or publ. Band.

"Festival March" (1921)
    ©: Band, Smith 17 Jan 1921; not ren.

"The Floral Parade" - march (1916)
    ©: Band, FBros 26 Jun 1916; ren FBros 8 Nov 1943.
        Orch, FBros 3 Dec 1918; ren FBros 19 Jly 1946.
        HPEBB, HPEOF.

"Florodora March" (1909)
    ©: Band, Wurlitzer 6 Mar 1909; not ren.

"Fort Chester" - march and two-step (1916)
    ©: Band, FBros 26 Jun 1916; ren FBros 8 Nov 1943.
        Orch, FBros 3 Dec 1918; ren FBros 19 Jly 1946.
        HPEBB, HPEOF.

"Fort Gay" - march (1913)
    ©: Band, FBros 1 Apr 1913; ren FBros 11 Oct 1940.
        Orch, FBros 21 Jan 1914; ren FBros 7 Jan 1942.
        WHBB, WHOF.

"Fort Royal" - march (1913)
    ©: Band, FBros 1 Apr 1913; ren FBros 11 Oct 1940.
        Orch, FBros 21 Jan 1914; ren FBros 7 Jan 1942.
        WHBB, WHOF.

"Georgiana" - waltzes (1916)
   ⓒ: Band, FBros 26 Jun 1916; ren FBros 8 Nov 1943.
      Orch, FBros 3 Dec 1918; ren FBros 19 Jly 1946.
      HPEBB, HPEOF.

"Golden Rod" - waltz (1913)
   ⓒ: Band, FBros 1 Apr 1913; ren FBros 11 Oct 1940.
      Orch, FBros 21 Apr 1914; ren FBros 7 Jan 1942.
      WHBB, WHOF.

"The Hippodrome" - march (1913)
   ⓒ: Band, FBros 1 Apr 1913; ren FBros 11 Oct 1940.
      Orch, FBros 21 Jan 1914; ren FBros 2 Jan 1942.
      WHBB, WHOF.

"Howard March" (1903)
   ⓒ: Band, Wurlitzer 24 Oct 1903; not ren.

"Ideal March" (no date)
   Not ⓒ or publ. Band.

"Ironclad" - march (1913)
   ⓒ: Band, FBros 1 Apr 1913; ren FBros 11 Oct 1940.
      Orch, FBros 21 Jan 1914; ren FBros 7 Jan 1942.
      WHBB, WHOF.

"Life and Liberty" - march (1908)
   ⓒ: Band, FBros 6 Sep 1908; not ren.

"The Lincoln March" (1909)
   ⓒ: Band, Wurlitzer 6 Mar 1909; not ren.

"Magneta" - overture (1913)
   ⓒ: Band, FBros 1 Apr 1913; ren FBros 11 Oct 1940.
      Orch, FBros 21 Jan 1914; ren FBros 7 Jan 1942.
      WHBB, WHOF.

"Majestic" - march (1915)
   Not ⓒ. Publ Smith. Band.

"March Endeavor" (1909)
   ⓒ: Band, FBros 1 Dec 1909; not ren.

"March Standard" (1922)
   Not ⓒ. Publ Smith. Band.

"Margaret Waltz" (1913)
   ⓒ: Band, FBros 1 Apr 1913; ren FBros 11 Oct 1940.
      Orch, FBros 21 Jan 1914; ren FBros 7 Jun 1942.
      WHBB, WHOF.

"The Mascot" - march (1913)
   Not ⓒ. Publ Star. Band; also orch.

"The Matinee" - march and two-step (1913)
   ⓒ: Band, FBros 1 Apr 1913; ren FBros 11 Oct 1940.
      Orch, FBros 21 Jan 1914; ren FBros 7 Jan 1942.
      WHBB, WHOF.

"Mazzini" - mazurka or three-step (1913)

Ⓒ: Band, FBros 1 Apr 1913; ren FBros 11 Oct 1940.
Orch, FBros 21 Jan 1914; ren FBros 7 Jan 1942.
WHBB, WHOF.

"Meaco Overture" (1921)
Not Ⓒ or publ. Band.

"Meaco Waltz" (1921)
Not Ⓒ or publ. Band.

"Melody to Youth" - serenade (1916)
Ⓒ: Band, FBros 26 Jun 1916; ren FBros 8 Nov 1943.
Orch, FBros 3 Dec 1918; ren FBros 19 Jly 1946.
HPEBB, HPEOF.

"Monogram March" (no date)
Not Ⓒ or publ. Band.

"Moonbeams" - serenade (1913)
Ⓒ: Band, FBros 1 Apr 1913; ren FBros 11 Oct 1940.
Orch, FBros 21 Jan 1914; ren FBros 7 Jan 1942.
WHBB, WHOF.

"Morning Leader" - march (1916)
Not Ⓒ. Publ. Smith. Band.

"The Night Riders" - patrol (1908)
Ⓒ: Band, FBros 21 Dec 1908; not ren.
Orch, same.

"Our Favorite Rag" - march and two-step (1913)
Ⓒ: Band, FBros 1 Apr 1913; ren FBros 11 Oct 1940.
Orch, FBros 21 Jan 1914; ren FBros 7 Jan 1942.
WHBB, WHOF.

"The Peerless" - march (1916)
Ⓒ: Band, FBros 26 Jun 1916; ren FBros 8 Nov 1943.
Orch, FBros 3 Dec 1918; ren FBros 19 Jly 1946.
HPEBB, HPEOF.

"The Poet's Dream" - serenade (1916)
Ⓒ: Band, FBros 26 Jun 1916; ren FBros 8 Nov 1943.
Orch, FBros 3 Dec 1918; ren FBros 19 Jly 1946.
HPEBB, HPEOF.

"The Premium" - march (1916)
Ⓒ: Band, FBros 26 Jun 1916; ren FBros 8 Nov 1943.
Orch, FBros 3 Dec 1918; ren FBros 19 Jly 1946.
HPEBB, HPEOF.

"Ragamuffin Rag" - march and two-step (1913)
Ⓒ: Band, FBros 6 Jan 1913; ren FBros 16 Sep 1940.
Orch, same.

"Rosida" - waltz (1916)
Ⓒ: Band, FBros 26 Jun 1916; ren FBros 8 Nov 1943.
Orch, FBros 3 Dec 1918; ren FBros 19 Jly 1916.
HPEBB, HPEOF.

"The Royal Pageant" - march and two-step (1913)
    ©: Band, FBros 1 Apr 1913; ren FBros 11 Oct 1940.
        Orch, FBros 21 Jan 1914; ren FBros 7 Jan 1942.
        WHBB, WHOF.

"A Rural Celebration" - descriptive piece (1909)
    ©: Band, FBros 28 Jun 1909; not ren.

"Salute to the Stars and Stripes" - march (1903)
    ©: Band, Wurlitzer 24 Oct 1903; not ren.
        Band (new arrangement), FBros 20 Jan 1942; not ren.

"Salute to Uncle Sam" - march (1908)
    ©: Band, FBros 28 Feb 1908; ren Will Huff 14 Feb 1936.

"Salute to Yoctangee 1925" - march (1925)
    Not © or publ. Band.

"Scioto Waltz" (1921)
    Not © or publ. Band.

"Screamer" - march (1918)
    Not ©. Publ Smith. Band.

"The Show Boy" - march (1911)
    ©: Band, FBros 4 Feb 1911; ren FBros 28 Jan 1939.
        Orch, FBros 14 Nov 1911; ren FBros 28 Jan 1939.

"The Show Girl" - march (1916)
    ©: Band, FBros 3 May 1916; ren FBros 8 Nov 1943.
        Orch, same.

"Southern Symphony" - serenade (no date)
    Not © or publ. Band.

"Square Deal" - march (1908)
    ©: Band, FBros 28 Aug 1908; not ren.

"The Squealer" - marchio circusosio (1912)
    ©: Band, FBros 8 Apr 1912; ren Will Huff 1 Nov 1939.

"Stilly Night" - serenade (1913)
    ©: Band, FBros 1 Apr 1913; ren FBros 11 Oct 1940.
        Orch, FBros 21 Jan 1914; ren FBros 7 Jan 1942.
        WHBB, WHOF.

"Tonophone Two Step" (1902)
    ©: Band, Wurlitzer 10 Mar 1902; not ren.

"A Trip to the Farm" - descriptive piece (1905)
    ©: Band, Wurlitzer 12 May 1905; not ren.

"The Troubadour" - waltz (1913)
    ©: Band, FBros 1 Apr 1913; ren FBros 11 Oct 1940.
        Orch, FBros 21 Jan 1914; ren FBros 7 Jan 1942.
        WHBB, WHOF.

"Troupers Triumphal" - march (1929)
    Not ©. Publ Star. Band.

"Tuxedo" - march (1916)
    ⓒ: Band, FBros 26 Jun 1916; ren FBros 8 Nov 1943.
       Orch, FBros 3 Dec 1918; ren FBros 19 Jly 1946.
       HPEBB, HPEOF.

"Victor" - march (probably 1912)
   Not ⓒ. Publ Star. Band; orch; also cornet solo with
       piano.

"Wireless Despatch" - march (1902)
    ⓒ: Band, Wurlitzer 20 Oct 1902; not ren.

"The Zouaves" - march (1913)
    ⓒ: Band, FBros 1 Apr 1913; ren FBros 11 Oct 1940.
       Orch, FBros 21 Jan 1914; ren FBros 7 Jan 1942.
       WHBB, WHOF.

"17th Regt. Band March" (1899)
    ⓒ: Band, Wurlitzer 24 Jly 1899; not ren.

BIBLIOGRAPHY

Bierley, Paul E. *Hallelujah Trombone !* Columbus, Ohio: Integrity Press, 1982.

Bierley, Paul E. "The Case of the Duplicate Composer." *Instrumentalist*, October, 1979.

Bachman, Harold. "Henry Fillmore: A Tribute to a Bandsman." *Music Journal*, December, 1968 (Part 1); January, 1969 (Part 2).

Kalfs, Barbara B. "Famed Composer Was Part of Early Adelphi Band." *Chillicothe* [Ohio] *Gazette*, October 13, 1973.

Autobiographical article by Will Huff, unpublished.

"Will Huff, an Appreciation." *Musical Messenger*, ca. May, 1913.

INDEX

58